Magic Research for Beginners

Questions, Experiments, Conclusions and Models

Knowledge ist the ability to give answers –

Wisdom is the art of asking questions.

Contact: www.HarryEilenstein.de
Harry.Eilenstein@web.de
Harry Eilenstein at youtube

Production and publishing house: BoD – Books on Demand, Norderstedt

ISBN: 9783754312650

Table of Contents

– the abbreviation "E" indicates an experiment –

I   How Does Research Work?

I 1.   General Principles of Research

If one wants to know whether magic is real or not, one must research it.

In order to do research in a sensible way, one must first be clear about what one is actually doing in research and what the results of research mean:

- One tries to see things as they actually are.

- This requires precise observation.

- Afterwards one looks for regularities and tries to formulate these as comprehensively as possible, without exceptions and generally valid – in such a way the "laws" and "formulas" develop.

Therefore, in research there is a certain sequence of activities, which can be found almost everywhere: "question – experiment – conclusion".

However, this simple, basic sequence has some more aspects and details, if we take a closer look:

1. **wondering**: Research starts with wondering about something, with a problem for which a solution is needed or similar.

2. **question**: A concrete question is derived from the wondering.

3. **known models**: One has a look at which possible answers to this question are already known, and whether there could be still further models.

4. **search for an experiment**: An experiment is searched for, with the help of which one can see more exactly the thing which one is investigating.

If there are several possible experiments, the simplest ones are chosen first and only then as secound experiment those that are probably the most effective ones – if these experiments should be clearly more complex.

5. **execution of the experiment**: The experiment is carried out. While doing so, all processes are closely observed and recorded.

Several things are important and conducive to this:
- the qualitative description
- the quantitative measurement
- the clear elaboration of the details

6. **explanatory model**: The smallest sufficient explanation is searched for, because it is the most probable.

If there are a very large number of possibilities, the most elegant, symmetric possibility is most likely to be the right one.

7. **probabilities**: Sometimes one does not find a clear result, but only probabilities. Also these probabilities should be investigated, observed and described as precisely as possible.

8. **importance of the model**: In many cases the smallest sufficient explanation for the observations can either confirm, refute or extend the previous general model for the whole area which one investigates. Possibly also a completely new model becomes necessary or new principles are recognized in this area.

9. **generality of the model**: By the principle proof of a thing it sometimes results that this proven thing must be present in many things and structures – which can lead under circumstances to a new interpretation and a new description of a whole area.

10. **verification of the conclusion**: It is often necessary to look at the conclusions again to see if one has really described the observations precisely or if one has possibly added unwittingly some assumptions.

11. **combination with other conclusions**: Sometimes the conclusion from one experiment can be combined with the conclusions from other experiments. This sometimes results in greater knowledge.

12. **contradictions**: Contradictions, where both sides of the contradiction can be clearly demonstrated as existing and real, allow the very big questions and insights: A situation that is contradictory in itself indicates that there is a higher, more comprehensive point of view from which this contradiction can be resolved.

13) **Comparison of structures**: A search is made for similarities between the structure found and other areas.

This is not in itself a proof of the correctness of the chosen descriptive model – but the existence of analogous structures in other domains makes an as yet unproven model more probable.

A structure that has been proven to occur in several places may help to better understand the subject currently under investigation.

14. **experience comparison**: The found results are compared with the observations and conclusions of other people and groups.

This sometimes results in new points of view, interpretations, classifications and models. Especially the deviations from the own observations are interesting, because they may indicate a "blind spot" in one's own experiments and interpretations.

15. **doubts**: Doubts arising in the experiment and in the conclusions drawn from it should be investigated as objectively and precisely as possible.

16. **questions**: In many cases new questions arise from the observations, conclusions and comparisons.

The conclusions should be checked experimentally as well as possible, so that one can be sure that they are correct.

17. **acclimatization**: After fundamental new discoveries and insights, a phase of acclimatization to the new point of view is often necessary.

18. **evaluation**: In the description of some observations there may be great subjective differences. These differences should also be worked out as clearly as possible and left as they are for the time being.

19. **use**: It makes sense to consider the results of one's own experiments also with regard to one's own extended possibilities of action and to use them or to make them generally known.

I 2.   Magic Research

The reason for being interested in the research of magic can be quite different:

- One wonders about the "green thumb" of one's own mother, who can make any plant bloom.

- One wonders how physics and astrology actually fit together.

- One has already experienced telepathy several times.

- There was a poltergeist in the house where you lived for half a year.
etc.

The reasons why one wants to get to the bottom of magic can be as different as the phenomena in magic – thus extremely colorful.

Now, of course, everyone will start his research from the phenomenon that has been the trigger for his own wondering. So there is an almost arbitrarily large number of ways in which one can explore magic.

For a book that cannot deal with every possible approach, it is advisable to proceed as generally as possible – in the hope that the questions of the readers will be taken up at some point in this "research journey into magic".

I 3.   One's Own Research

If you want to do your own research and expand your worldview to include the possibilities of magic, you can certainly read a few books on the subject. However, a book is never a solid basis for one's own world view, only one's own experiences.

Therefore, one should also use this book, that you are currently holding in your hands, primarily as a stimulus for your own experiments.

Also the conclusions presented in this book should be checked – maybe you draw quite different conclusions from the experimental results yourself. The probability for this is quite great – already because each humans regards the world from a somewhat different angle, which is coined among other things by one's own Horoskop.

Nevertheless, it is quite probable that gradually a ground-set of knowledge is formed, which is common to all magical worldviews – even if this knowledge receives a different "coloring" and evaluation in each worldview.

I 4. What Is Magic?

A large part of magic consists in creating an effect in the world that originates from consciousness. So it can't be completely wrong to first take a closer look at the relationship between consciousness and matter.

II   What Is Consciousness?

II 1.   How Do Matter And Consciousness Relate To Each Other?

If one wants to examine what consciousness is, one must necessarily also examine its relationship to matter – they are the two elements whose relationship is at stake in magic.

For the relation of consciousness and matter to each other there are two old and one newer model:

Model 1: Consciousness is a by-product of matter and is purely subjective and has no reality in itself.

This is the usual scientific view. From this point of view the consciousness is only a "substanc-less, subjective mirage".

Model 2: Consciousness is the only real thing; all matter is nothing but contents in consciousness.

This is a widespread religious and philosophical view. From this point of view the world is only an illusion ("maya").

Model 3: The world is the outside of reality; consciousness is the inside of reality. Both are a view of the same reality – just viewed in two different ways.

This is a model that can be derived from experiences with magic, astrology, religion, and the Kabbalistic Tree of Life.

These three models have three things in common, without which one could not describe the relationship between consciousness and matter:

Statement 1: There is both consciousness and matter.

Statement 2: Consciousness and matter are two different things.

Statement 3: Consciousness and matter affect each other and are consequently connected with each other.

      a) Consciousness acts on matter: I can decide to put a strawberry in my mouth.

      a) Matter acts on consciousness: I can perceive the taste of the strawberry I am eating.

12

The following graphic shows the simplest model that connects these three statements and represents them graphically:

Model 1: Consciousness and Matter
Consciousness
↕
Matter

II 2. How Is Consciousness Constructed?

To understand magic, it is helpful to first understand consciousness better.

For this consideration an experiment is necessary, that however is not the simplest of all experiments:

Experiment 1
This experiment consists in becoming inwardly silent.
To achieve this, it is easiest to meditate once with someone who can already do this. This state corresponds to deep sleep – so you can sometimes experience it when you wake up not from a dream, but from deep sleep. In this state one is only consciousness, which is aware of itself – without any content.

Three elements of consciousness can be distinguished:

1ˢᵗ element: The most obvious element is the contents of consciousness: the thoughts, the feelings, the perceptions and the memories.

2ⁿᵈ element: The basic element is consciousness itself. One can stop thinking, feeling, perceiving and remembering something. By this one reaches a state of just being conscious of being conscious. This state of "inner silence" is like the canvas on which one may paint a picture, like the clay from which one may form a sculpture, like the silence in which a melody may sound …

3ʳᵈ element: The most unknown element are the boundaries of consciousness. In one's own waking consciousness there is only little information at one's disposal, and also only few of the thoughts one could think are really thought. The same applies to the feelings and to the memories.

Finally, there is also a boundary of consciousness which, so to speak, runs all around a person and "envelops" him. This border of consciousness has the effect that one does not constantly perceive what all people around one are thinking or feeling.

With this information one can extend the consciousness/matter medell around the consciousness contents and around the consciousness border outwardly:

Model 2: The Structure of Consciousness
Consciousness – with or without contents
↕ (boundary of consciousness) ↕
Matter

II 3.   What Types Of Contents Of Consciousness Are There?

The contents of consciousness can be divided into four or five clearly distinguishable groups:

1. perceptions: Perception creates an image of what is perceived in the consciousness. By this one becomes aware of one's environment.
Perception looks into the present.

2. memories: The contents of the conscious mind are "stored" and can be retrieved when needed. Among other things, the judgment of a situation and the ability to learn are based on this.
The memory looks in the past.

3. feelings: Feelings are impulses – they have a direction but no measure. They serve to evaluate perceptions. These evaluations enable action that is conducive to one's well-being.
Feelings look to the present.

4. thoughts: Thoughts are structures – they have a measure but no direction. They serve to compare events. This makes general statements about the world possible, which then in turn serve as a standard for one's own actions. Thinking makes planning possible.
Thinking looks into the future.

In addition to these four elements of consciousness, which are on approximately the same level, there is a fifth element that is superior to these four elements:

5. will: The will is the center – all impulses emanate from it. It directs the perception, the memory, the feelings and the thinking.
The will looks into the past, into the present and into the future.

Model 3: The types of the contents of consciousness
Consciousness with contents of consciousness: Will ⇕   ⇕ Thoughts ⇔ Feelings ⇕   ⇕ Memories ⇕ Perceptions
↕
Matter

II 4.   What Are The Types Of Consciousness?

There are at least four different types of consciousness.

- **waking consciousness**: Waking consciousness is the consciousness that is present while awake. It makes the decisions.
This consciousness can be thought of as an office where all information relevant to the momentary situation arrives and is processed.

- **ecstasy state**: The ecstasy state occasionally occurs when a situation becomes more extreme, i.e. when the waking consciousness is characterized by lust, fear, greed or by a high level of concentration. Consequently, ecstasy occurs during orgasm, panic, meditation, etc. Traumas can also lead to a "negative ecstasy", in which the waking consciousness of the person concerned becomes "blind", so to speak, to the variety of the situation and the possibilities in it. The state of ecstasy is completely focused on a single content of consciousness. In the case of focussing an a trauma one would rather say "fixated" instead of "focused".
The ecstatic state can be thought of as the bright lamp on the desk in the office of the waking consciousness, illuminating with a spotlight only what is most important at that moment.

- **subconsciousness**: The subconscious contains all information, all perceptions, all memories. This information is charged with more or less emotions or is completely neutral. They are ordered by associations, i.e. the memories on a subject are all linked together and in this way form a symbol that can be experienced, for example, in a dream – which is why this consciousness can also be called dream-consciousness.
The subconsciousness can be seen as an well-ordered archive, which sends the data to the office, which are requested from there, because they are needed in the momentary situation. The archive can also send information to the office on its own initiative.

- **deep sleep**: The deep sleep consciousness is empty, without content – it is only aware of itself. This consciousness is the "canvas" on which the contents of consciousness are "painted".
This consciousness can be imagined as the house where the archive of the subconsciousness, the office of the waking consciousness and the desk lamp of ecstasy are located.

These four forms of consciousness can be distinguished on the one hand by the number of their consciousness contents and on the other hand by their EEG frequency (frequency of the electric brain waves):

Overview 1: The four forms of consciousness		
Consciousness	*Number of contents*	*EEG frequency*
deep sleep	none	∅ 3 Hz (2 - 4 Hz)
subconscious mind	all	∅ 6 Hz (4 - 8 Hz)
waking consciousness	some (those that are relevant)	∅ 12 Hz (8 - 16 Hz)
ecstasy	only one	∅ 24 Hz (16 - 32 Hz)

There is obviously a meaningful division of labor in consciousness: deep sleep is the foundation; the subconscious mind holds all information; the waking consciousness coordinates all information relevant to the momentary situation; and the ecstasy consciousness brings content to the center when needed.

These four consciousnesses can be represented by a simple model:

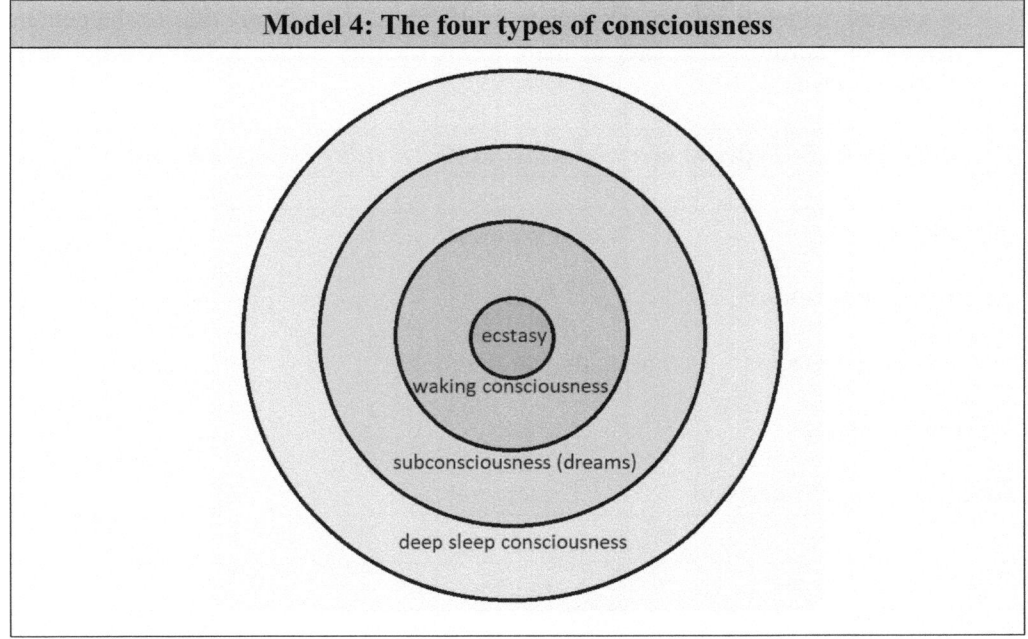

Model 4: The four types of consciousness

ecstasy

waking consciousness

subconsciousness (dreams)

deep sleep consciousness

These four types of consciousness can be summarized with the graph representing the types of consciousness contents. To be able to do this, we can look at the four types of the contents of consciousness again:

1. **<u>Perception</u>** happens in the subconscious and is passed on to the waking consciousness when needed.
The same is true for **<u>memory</u>**.

2. **<u>Thinking</u>** happens in the waking consciousness – it is something to be done in the waking consciously. The reference point of thought is the world that thought tries to understand. Thoughts are stored in the subconscious mind. The subconscious mind itself does not think, instead it sorts and arranges its contents by associations, i.e. it puts similar things together into a complex.

3. **<u>Feelings</u>** happen in the waking consciousness. Feelings are the evaluation of a perception. So they express what one wants, how one finds something. The starting point of feelings is therefore one's own character, one's own being, one's own will – they are the inner impulses that push into the world. The feelings, like everything else, are stored in the subconscious.

4. The **<u>will</u>** is that in man which wants to express itself, which wants to radiate, which wants to experience itself. Thus, the will belongs to the center, to the innermost character of man, to his identity – that is, to the deep sleep consciousness.

Model 5: Types of consciousness and contents of consciousness
deep sleep: Consciousness
waking consciousness: Will
⇕   ⇕
waking consciousness: Thoughts ⇔ Feelings
⇕   ⇕
subconsciousness: Memories
⇕
subconsciousness / ecstasy: Perceptions
↕
Matter

II 5. Where Does A Magical Effect Take Place?

In the usual world model, the interactions are all physical interactions:

    - All perceptions come into consciousness via the senses;

    - all resolutions come into the world through the body; and

    - every effects originate from a body and act on a body.

This gives rise to the following interaction model:

Model 6: The usual interactions		
Person A		Person B
Consciousness		Consciousness
⇕		⇕
Body	⇔	Body

The (inter-)actions of magic, which have not yet been proven in this book, start from the consciousness of person A and act directly on person B or a thing outside of person A. The previous graphic must therefore be supplemented by an arrow, which starts from the consciousness of person A and goes directly out into the world. At first it is not quite clear where this arrow leads exactly – to the consciousness or to the body of person B.

Model 7: The presumed "magic interactions model"		
Person A		Person B
Consciousness	⇔	Consciousness
⇕		⇕
Body	⇔	Body

II 6.   What Is The Relationship Between The Different States Of Consciousness?

These four forms of consciousness can be coordinated with each other in various ways – this is the very activity of a meditator by which he can achieve "altered states of consciousness. This coordination of different forms of consciousness with each other is what a meditator does in the "land of consciousness" while he is traveling there.

This coordination is like tuning an instrument – after meditation everything is in its right place, in the right state and organically connected with everything else.

So meditation is actually something very simple – even though there are a lot of different varieties of methods.

Each of the four modes of consciousness has a certain frequency, which form octaves to each other (double frequency):

deep sleep	- ∅ 3 Hz (2 - 4 Hz)
dream consciousness	- ∅ 6 Hz (4 - 8 Hz)
waking consciousness	- ∅ 12 Hz (8 - 16 Hz)
ecstasy	- ∅ 24 Hz (16 - 32 Hz)

One can imagine the processes during meditation as a tuning of two consciousness frequencies to each other. In a dream journey, for example, two vibrations of the waking consciousness (12 Hz = 12 vibrations per second) would vibrate together in harmony with one vibration of the subconsciousness (6 Hz = 6 vibrations per second). Two vibrations of the waking consciousness take the same time as one vibration of the subconsciousness. Or in the langue of music: the waking consciousness vibrates in quarter-notes and the subconsiousness in half notes – because two quarter notes are exactly as long as one half note, the two "melodies" of the waking consciousness and the subconsciousness fit together.

The vibration of the waking consciousness is not always exactly an octave of the vibration of the subconsciousness – they may be e.g. 5Hz and 14Hz. The "work" of meditation consists of the slight changing of these frequencies for example to 6Hz and 12Hz and thus to octaves – now the waking consciousness and the subconsciousness vibrate together.

This "vibrating together" is the effect of meditation: harmony, strength, centering, integration, support etc.

This connection can be clarified most simply by a diagram:

Overview 2: The mode of action of meditation										
uncoordinated rhythm (normal consciousness)										
deep sleep										
dream										
waking										
ecstasy										
coordinated rhythm (meditation)										
deep sleep										
dream										
waking										
ecstasy										

The different states of consciousness result mainly from the coordination of two forms of consciousness with each other. One of the forms involved is always the waking consciousness – simply because this combination of consciousness forms would otherwise not be conscious.

II 6. a)   Waking consciousness

Waking consciousness has as its quality the presence in the here and now. This presence can be rather nebulous or quite clear. One can "be completely here" or drift to a good part in memories, fears, hopes, etc. and notice only little of the world.

II 6. b)   Waking consciousness and dream consciousness

When the waking consciousness is combined with the subconscious (dream consciousness), the waking consciousness goes out of its office into the archive and looks around.

This happens in a daydream, for example, when one is traveling by train and looks out of the window and completely sinks into the memory of the last vacation and again feels the sand on the beach under the soles of one's feet – or when one wakes up from a dream in the morning and the dream continues to run in its own dynamics for another ten seconds and one watches consciously as if in the cinema.

You can also specifically go into this state and then look at the information about a subject in your own subconscious – this is then called "dream journey", "trance journey", "fantasy journey", "shamanic journey", etc.

The subconscious mind has the ability to obtain external information by telepathy and to cause external effects by telekinesis (this is shown later on by experiments). Therefore, the dream journey is a practical way to use telepathy and telekinesis specifically.

Another effect of the coordination between the waking consciousness and the subconsciousness is the perception of the life force. One can say somewhat simplified that the subconsciousness corresponds to one's own life force body ("astral body"). Therefore, for example, the perception of the aura is also connected with this coordination of waking consciousness and subconsciousness.

In this state one also perceives the aliveness (life force) of plants and animals – not always as an outer glow, but sometimes also as an inner glow: One sees the aliveness even of stones and perceives their essence. When one is in this state, one can be completely taken by the sight of a blade of grass. In this state, everything looks as if you are seeing it for the first time in your life – although at the same time the memories of previous experiences may be present.

In this state, the purely concentrative "Be here now!" becomes an intense experience of life – then one doesn't need to concentrate on the "here and now" anymore … one is completely seized by the here and now. Then one is really alive.

On dream journeys as well as in this "striken state" it is quite easy to speak e.g. also with plants, animals, stones, deities etc. and to receive from them also gifts – from visions over realizations up to healings and joy of life.

II 6. c)   Waking consciousness and deep sleep

Since deep sleep is a form of consciousness without content, the combination of waking consciousness with deep sleep consciousness creates an inner silence: one is simply consciousness that is aware of itself.

This may sound rather boring, but it is not – on the contrary: in this state one experiences a formless abundance, an richness, a glow and a warmth that spreads from within. One begins to smile like the Buddha statues or the ancient Egyptian statues. One is happy for no reason.

II 6. d)   Waking consciousness and ecstasy

The combination of the waking state and ecstasy is of a slightly different nature than the two combinations of two states of consciousness already described. This is because the waking consciousness is not normally aware of the subconscious and deep sleep consciousness – ecstasy consciousness, on the other hand, arises from the narrowing of the focus of the waking consciousness from several contents of consciousness to a single thing. Thus, one is always awake in ecstasy.

Consequently, the question is how to get into this state. In everyday life, this usually happens by pleasure or fear – that is, for example, during orgasm and in a panic attack.

However, one can also reach this state by concentrating on an image, on a mantra, on a movement, a deity, etc. in meditation. While the ecstasies that arise out of desire or fear urge action as quickly as possible, the ecstasy that arises out of meditation rests in itself – there is nothing in this ecstasy that one needs to do.

In Kundalini Yoga and Tantra, sexuality is indeed used in meditation, but since it is only the "fire" that sets an inner process in motion and is not aimed at the experience of pleasure, a state that rest in itselve also arises in Kundalini and Tantra meditations and rituals.

II 6. e)   Waking Consciousness, Dream Consciousness, and Deep Sleep

It is obviously possible (and natural) to coordinate not only two states of consciousness, but also several states of consciousness at once. However, there are hardly any systematic instructions for this. The most important of them is the mandala meditation, which is often connected with contemplations and rituals. A mandala used for this purpose consists of at least two circular rings and one circle:

- The outermost circular ring symbolizes the body and the waking consciousness,

- the middle circle symbolizes the psyche and the subconscious, and

- the inner circle symbolizes the identity (soul) and deep sleep consciousness.

By contemplations (outer circle ring), dream journeys (middle circle ring) and stillness meditations (inner circle), a picture is built up in which all three forms of consciousness have their place and eventually attune and coordinate with each other. This is a rather complex and somewhat lengthy process.

II 6. f) Waking Consciousness, Dream Consciousness, Deep Sleep, and Ecstasy

In coordinating all four forms of consciousness, a mandala with three circular rings and one circle is used:

- The outermost circular ring symbolizes the body and the waking consciousness,

- the middle circular ring symbolizes the psyche and the subconsciousness,

- the inner circular ring symbolizes the inner man and woman united physically and the state of ecstasy, and

- the inner circle represents the identity (soul) and the deep sleep consciousness.

By contemplations (outer circle), dream journeys (middle circle), tantric rituals as a couple (inner circle) and stillness meditations (inner circle), a picture is built up in which all four forms of consciousness have their place and finally attune and coordinate with each other.

II 6. g) Overview

In the following table the possible types of consciousness coordination are shown on the left. The dark areas in the respective line show which types of consciousness are coordinated in the process.

Overview 3: The Forms of Consciousness Coordination				
	deep sleep	*subconsciousness*	*waking*	*ecstasy*
waking			■	
dream journey		■	■	
silence mediation	■		■	
ecstasy meditation			■	■
mandala	■	■	■	
mandala ecstasy	■	■	■	■

III   Can Magic be Proven?

In the "normal" psyche of a human being and in his "normal" life there are two fundamentally different processes: perception and action. Perception comes from the outside in and action goes from the inside out.

These two processes are also found in magic: the magic perception is called "telepathy" and the magic action is called "telekinesis".

So, in a first step, it is about the fundamental proof that telepathy and telekinesis exist.

III 1.   Does Telepathy Exist?

In order to clarify this question, different experiments can be performed. The two experiments described in this chapter are two basic experiments that everybody knows or can perform.

III 1. a)   Unconscious telepathy

Experiment 2
The simplest proof of telepathy is a phenomenon that almost everybody knows: Almost every human being senses when he is being stared at from behind. This telepathic ability dates back to the Paleolithic Age and was necessary for survival at that time when a hungry tiger snucked up on us.

From this observation two interesting things can be concluded:

1. **ability of the subconscious**: Telepathy is coupled to the instincts and must not be carried out consciously. This suggests that this ability is a part of the subconsciousness and not of the waking consciousness. This is also plausible in that deep sleep consciousness is devoid of content, ecstasy consciousness has only a single content, and waking consciousness contains only the content that is allowed to pass through to waking consciousness from perception and memory by the selection mechanisms because it is relevant to the momentary situation.

The normal physical sensory perceptions also pass through the subconsciousness into the waking consciousness. Therefore it is not surprising that this also applies to telepathic perception – all perceptions run the same way.

2) **interaction of consciousness**: In the normal physical model there are three interactions:

> a) The consciousness acts on its body;
>
> b) the body acts on its consciousness; and
>
> c) the body acts on other bodies.

The "staring phenomenon" shows, however, that there is also a direct interaction between consciousness (human being) and consciousness (tiger):

> a) The human being feels the consciousness of the hungry tiger.
>
> b) It would be however also conceivable that the human being does not feel the consciousness of the tiger, but the physical presence of the tiger.

Since the consciousness of the tiger is however firmly connected with his body, both interpretations do not make a big difference: The physical presence and the intention of the tiger in his consciousness are perceived by the consciousness of the human being whom the tiger stares at. From where exactly the information arrives in the consciousness of the human being (from the body or from the consciousness of the tiger), remains unclear for the time being.

The ususal, non-magical model of mind and body extended by telepathy looks now as follows:

Model 8: Telepathy as an effect		
Man		*Tiger*
Consciousness	⇨ ⇨	Consciousness
⇕	⬂	⇕
Consciousness	⇔	Consciousness

It is also not clear at first what kind of "movement" telepathy is:

- Is it an extension of the consciousness of the human being to the tiger?

- Does the tiger send out something that comes to the consciousness of the human being?

- Or is the model of the movement "from A to B" for the telepathy inapplicable?

III 1. b)   Conscious telepathy

There is also a telepathy experiment which can be performed deliberately. It is based on the assumption that the telepathic perceptions come from the subconsciousness into the waking consciousness. If one tries to perceive something telepathically, one does not know at first whether the perceived thing is really a telepathic perception or only an inner picture, an association.

The following experiment makes it possible to distinguish between both.

Experiment 3

Ideally, a whole school class or a similarly large group participates in this experiment. For the experiment, ten to twenty different postcards with striking motifs are needed. These postcards are placed individually in envelopes, which are sealed so that the postcards are no longer visible.

Now the class is divided into groups of four. Each group sits at a table and receives an envelope that is placed in the middle of the table. Now everyone concentrates for about three minutes on the postcard in the envelope and then writes down all impressions on a piece of paper – this writing down is necessary so that no one adds anything to their perceptions or leaves anything out afterwards.

Then the perceptions are compared. The things that all four or at least three of the four persons have perceived are obviously telepathic perceptions, because that four people have the same association that does not refer to the postcard is extremely unlikely.

Now, if the four students perceived, for example, "a lot of blue," "warmth," "noise," and a "yellow spot," that sounds a lot like a beach scene with sunshine.

Now you can fill in this framework with the things that two of the four students saw. For example, if one student saw a tree and one student saw a palm tree, there will probably also be a palm tree on the beach picture.

The perceptions that are only associations, i.e. "noise", are different for each of the four students and fall out of the description of the telepathically seen picture in this procedure.

Of course, this experiment can also be done simply with four students, but if six groups or more recognize their image correctly at the same time, this has a much greater persuasive power ...

In this experiment, telepathy is directed on a hidden object and not on a "tiger" with consciousness. From the three possible connections with which one can describe the "staring phenomenon", consequently, the possibility falls away that the postcard sends something. So, there remain the "extending of the consciousness of the human being to the postcard" and the possibly still unknown connection, which does not consist in a "movement".

III 1. c)   Summary: Telepathy

These two experiments show that there is both conscious and unconscious telepathy. So there are two different cases:

- The telepathic information arrives in the subconscious mind and can then be passed on by it possibly as "situation-relevant information" immediately into the waking consciousness (hungry tiger).

- The waking consciousness wants to know something and instructs the subconsciousness with a telepathic search, whereupon the subconsciousness carries out this order and sends the results to the waking consciousness (postcard picture).

III 2. Does Telekinesis Exist?

Telekinesis is the "moving of objects by will". In an extended sense, other forms of changing the material world by the will would also belong to telekinesis, such as freezing water, invulnerability to fire, levitation, increasing 5 loaves of bread to 100 loaves of bread, and the like.

But first of all it is about the basic proof of telekinesis.

III 2. a) Simple paper wheel

Experiment 4

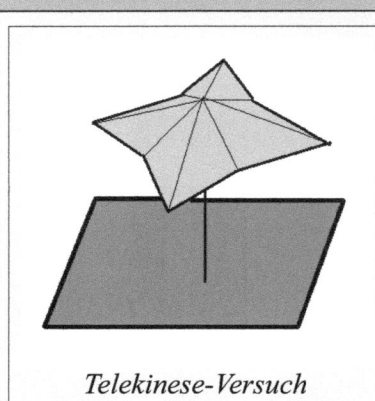

Telekinese-Versuch

For this experiment you need a piece of cardboard, a pin and a piece of paper, which is 4cm·4cm large.

Put the pin through the cardboard so that the pin is stuck vertically with the point upwards in the cardboard, which is lying on the table or on the floor. Bend the paper slightly in the two diagonals and in the two lines that divide the square piece of paper into two equal rectangles, so that the center of the piece of paper can be placed on the needle without falling off.

Then you hold a hand at a short distance next to the paper wheel and turn it by telekinesis – videos about this experiment may be found on youtube under "telekinesis paper wheel" or "PSI-wheel".

The actual telekinesis consists of wanting and imagining that the paper wheel turns. However, this should not degenerate into strained or tense concentration. You can also do this experiment with several people – and if they laugh during doing this experiment (as is often the case with doing something completely new), it is even easier.

With some people the attempt works immediately, some must forst have a look at videos, and again others must have demonstrated to them first.

Thus, telepathy and telekinesis (if the experiments were successful) are now proven.

III 2. b)   Summary: telepathy and telekinesis

Telepathy and telekinesis can be proven by two simple experiments (postcard and paper wheel).

Telepathy is a form of perception of the subconscious. It can be exercised independently by the subconscious, but it can also be done consciously by the waking consciousness.

IV   Can Telepathy be Described more Precisely?

After the basic proof that there is magic perception (telepathy) as well as magic effect (telekinesis), the question arises, how these two processes work exactly and what are their possibilities.

IV 1.   What Happens During Telepathy?

Telepathy is sometimes translated as "mind reading". However, the following experiments and conclusions show that telepathy is much more differentiated and diverse than "mind-reading" and that it also does not primarily refer to thoughts. Moreover, it can look quite divers and can occur in the most divers situations.

IV 1. a)   Hypnosis

In hypnosis an interesting phenomenon occurs: The hypnotist turns off the waking consciousness of the hypnotized and puts himself in the place of the waking consciousness of the hypnotized. The hypnotist can do this by words, by gestures or just by his concentration.

Experiment 5
Person A hypnotizes person B by making person B look at a swinging pendulum in person A's hand and telling him that person B is relaxing, that his body is getting heavy and warm, that he is getting tired and falling asleep.
Detailed instructions may be found in my book "Hypnosis for Beginners".

In this experiment there is no direct evidence of telepathy, but it is a process in which the consciousness of person A massively intervenes in the consciousness of person B.

IV 1. b)   Remote hypnosis

There is also a hypnosis experiment in which the involvement of telepathy is not unmistakable:

Experiment 6
Person A, who is trained in hypnosis, stands in his room and hypnotizes person B, who is in a completely different place. Person A conducts this hypnotizing as if person B were standing or sitting in front of her. Thereupon person B (who may be miles away) falls into hypnosis and does what person A tells her to do.

In remote hypnosis, the "extension of consciousness" to the hypnotized person is unmistakable. The hypnotist also perceives hypnotizing as such an extension of his own consciousness to the consciousness of the hypnotized.

Thus, telepathy can be described as an "extension of one's own waking consciousness to the waking consciousness of another person."

Model 9: Telepathy as a hypnosis tool		
Human being		*Human being*
Consciousness	⇨	Consciousness
⇕		⇕
Body	⇔	Body

Since the subconscious mind has a direct access to the telepathy ability (as it has the direct access to the sense perceptions) telepathy can be done by the waking consciousness (postcard experiment, remote hypnosis), but the subconscious mind can also carry out the telepathy independently (feeling the staring of the tiger).

Just as one constantly sees, hears, touches, tastes and smells all sorts of things, the subconscious mind apparently allows telepathic perception to roam as well. When something important is perceived by the physical senses or by the telepathic faculty, the subconsciousness sends this information to the waking consciousness as an image or as a "disturbance".

IV 1. c) Hypnosis Game

If you sometimes play "City, land, river" etc. with your children, you can try a special variation of this game.

Experiment 7
Person A asks person B a question, e.g. "What is the capital of Australia?" Person A concentrates intensely on "Sydney" and tries to get person B to say "Sydney" even though person B knows that "Canberra" would be correct.   This game works best when Person B knows nothing about what Person A is doing.
In this guessing game, of course, Person B can conversely try to recognize the answer in person A's conscious mind, if he doesn't know the answer.   (I played this this game very often with a lot of fun with my son when he was young – he is now very fit with telepathy.)

In this game, I have experienced the most amazing things when I have asked children complicated things that are far outside the realm of general knowledge and that the children had never thought about before.
  For example, I once asked my son why, two days after the new moon, you can see not only the thin crescent moon, but also, very faintly, the whole round moon. He said immediately without hesitation that the light of the sun is reflected by the earth to the moon and illuminates him – like also the full moon illuminates the earth.
  I suppose that he took this information telepathically out of my mind.

This game shows that there can be straight "telepathic conversations". The consciousness is obviously able to perceive also the actions of another consciousness (e.g. the concentration on a wrong answer).

36

IV 1. d)   Hypnosis fight

Experiment 8
Two people sit down in front of each other and try to hypnotize the other, i.e. to put the other to sleep, without words or gestures. A wide variety of imaginations can be used: the other person gets tired, his power flows into the earth, his eyes become heavy, he is wrapped in a black blanket, you interrupt the life force flow of his kundalini, you stop the natural rotation of the other person's chakras, he falls asleep as a baby in his mother's arms, he lies dead in a coffin, etc.

There is no other experiment that makes the processes of hypnosis and telepathy clear to this extend – one feels the pressure of the other's will, one sees the images the other uses, one experiences which of one's own countermeasures are effective and which are not, etc.

IV 1. e)   The hiding experiment

The following experiment can also be done with children. After two or three attempts, however, one should first play something else with the children, so that no "telepathy fatigue" occurs.

Experiment 9
Person A is hiding. Person B searches for him internally, i.e. telepathically. Person B probably finds person A.
Person A hides and imaginatively conceals himself in a "fog". Person B finds person A only when searching for such a fog.
Person A hides and focuses on another place. Person B finds person A only by searching inwardly for the place that feels most unobtrusive, boring, unlikely, etc.

Here the telepathic abilities of two people make a little competition. This shows that one can expand one's own consciousness not only perceptively, but also formatively – which has already been shown in hypnosis.

In a Viking saga it is reported about two sorcerers, who tracked down the whereabouts of another sorcerer by looking over the whole land and searching for a place where there is a fog, because of which they cannot recognize what is in this place.

IV 1. f) Dream journeys in pairs

Experiment 10

I have often made dream journeys in pairs on a subject that interested both of us. In almost every dream journey the effect occurred several times that I saw something and that the other person began to describe it before I had said anything about it. The same happened also in reverse.
    The perceptions that both saw independently of each other were often not just simple things like "I see a tree." but also more exotic things like "Hm, I see a dragon – and it has a bandage on its left front paw."
    This effect also occurs in group dream journeys with more than two people.

These experiences clearly show that both dream travelers are in the same vision.

During such dream journeys, people talk to each other while they are on the way – similar to talking while taking a hike through a valley together.

Such joint dream journeys can also be undertaken by four or five people – but with even more people it gradually becomes confusing, for too much people something and want to say something. Also in these group dream journeys everyone is in the same picture and experiences the same things.

So there is a "telepathy coordination".

IV 1. g) Family constellations

The currently best known form of group telepathy is probably the systemic family constellation. In this, a group of people meet to seek healing.

Experiment 11
The person seeking healing tells what situation they are in. The leader of the constellation then decides which people are important in the story of the person seeking healing – e.g. himself, his parents, his wife and his son. Then the other participants are asked who would like to represent these people.   These people then all place themselves in a designated area in the room (e.g. on a large carpet) and see what they intuitively want to do. It quickly becomes apparent that these "actors" are actually connected to the persons they represent, because although they know next to nothing about the persons they represent, they speak like the persons they represent, are choleric like them, limp like them, etc..
In a family constellation, the entire situation of the person seeking healing is, so to speak, telepathically summoned and intuitively staged by the "actors".   Not only people, but also parts of the psyche of the person seeking advice, the planets from his horoscope, his hometown and everything else can be set up in this way.
There are also "involuntary mini family constellations". This happens when one is with a person and is drawn into a role that the other person has in him or her because of their past experiences. Then you start to behave differently than you normally would – but usually you only notice this if you are quite attentive to what you want, feel, think and do.

IV 1. h) Mass panic

Mass psychosis, mass panic and similar phenomena can also be counted among the phenomena of collective telepathy. However, these phenomena are not suitable for proving telepathy per se, since they can be also explained without telepathy – though these explanations are not entirely convincing.

However, these phenomena become more understandable, if one has already proved telepathy and therefore adds it to the explanation: When a sufficiently large number of people feel or imagine the same thing, a telepathic pull or current is created which draws almost all other people into these feelings and imaginings.

IV 1. i) Telepathic cooperation

My son David works at the GSI ("GSI Helmholz Centre for Heavy Ion Research") in Darmstadt and develops image processing procedures for different experiments that are carried out there. We talk from time to time about what he is doing there and what possible solutions he has discovered – even though I cannot follow him on the programming level, but only on the general level, since I myself have not learned programming.

Some months ago I woke up and already in my dream I had started to think about a problem I had noticed in my dream with electronic image processing. I thought about this problem for about an hour and a half (which I usually never do). After this I did something else.

Two days later I talked to David on the phone and told him about my thoughts and my ideas for a solution. He told me that he had also discovered this problem and had been thinking about it for a few days and that he had found the solution that very morning at the time when also I myself had stopped thinking about it.

Did I simply hear telepathically quite precisely what David was thinking about, or did we couple our two consciousnesses to solve the problem together?

The group dream journeys show that there is such a telepathic coordination of inner images – why shouldn't we be able to use it to solve problems?

IV 1. j) Summary: telepathy possibilities

The previous experiments show that telepathy is not only a simple perception of a single piece of information, but that complex interactions can be created.

The question games show that one can spontaneously take over a special knowledge from another person. There is even the joint telepathic solution of a problem.

The group dream journeys and the family constellation show very clearly that several people can also be telepathically coordinated with each other as a group. So there are at least "telepathic conference circuits". However, not only the images that the persons involved see are coordinated, but also what they perceive together – e.g. a place unknown to them, which they view during a dream journey.

By the various hypnosis experiments one can prove two things:

    1. Hypnosis is mainly based on telepathy and

    2. The waking consciousness of a person has the possibility to telepathically interfere with the waking consciousness of another person and even to switch off the waking consciousness of this person.

    Against these interferences the other one can defend himself of course and even proceed for his part to the attack, whereby a "telepathic fight" arises.

    The so-called "battle of wills" between two people for dominance in a situation is probably such a "telepathic battle". Dominant people are apparently particularly good at this form of struggle.

IV 2.   Is There "Animal Telepathy"?

IV 2. a)   The dog experiment

One can ask whether only humans are able to perform telepathy or whether animals can do it, too.

Experiment 12
One imagines alone or with several people a white rabbit in front of the nose of a dog, which lies there and rests. This experiment produces entertaining results …
This game can also be done with a mouse in front of a cat. With horses, one must rather take pictures of a threat. There are many creative possibilities here.

The effect of the dog experiment clearly shows that animals are susceptible to telepathy.

IV 2. b)   The 100th monkey

Experiment 13
On an island near Japan, monkeys were fed potatoes. After a while, one monkey discovered that the potatoes were more pleasant to eat if he washed them in the stream beforehand. Little by little, some monkeys imitated him. This imitation effect was quite slow at first, but when a certain number of monkeys had learned to wash the potatoes, suddenly all the monkeys did it – and all the monkeys on all the other islands, too, who could not have perceived this discovery directly.
This is, so to speak, a peaceful variant of the dynamics in a mass panic – when a certain number of people want, feel, think, see or do the same thing, all people do it at once.

Similar collective phenomena can be observed in animals in the wild. They often change their behavior collectively. However, it is generally not possible to determine whether this is due to telepathy or imitation.

Such changes are e.g. the escape distance of buzzards, which has shrunk massively from over 100m to often less than 10m some years ago, or the occurrence of jays in groups, which has become more frequent since about 15 years.

Here a quantitative telepathy phenomenon is observable. It takes "100 monkeys" to get a "telepathy avalanche" rolling. Obviously, a behavior must be tried, tested and found to be good by a sufficient number of individuals to turn on the common "telepathic broadcast" that this kind of behavior is good.

This phenomenon confirms the assumption that telepathy does not only consist of single "telepathy threads" between single humans, animals, plants and things, but that the single telepathy event is a part of a larger "organism", in which the single telepathy event is a "cell", so to speak.

IV 2. c) Swarm Consciousness

If one looks for collective telepathy in animals, one also finds the "swarm consciousness" of some animal species. It is conceivable (and probable) that telepathy also plays a role in this, but it is not directly detectable in this case.

However, if one has proved telepathy with animals (dog experiment) and also collective telepathy ("100th monkey"), it would be nonsensical to assume that with the swarm behavior, i.e. the simultaneous same movements of all animals no telepathy would participate. The animals will always use all the abilities they have …

IV 2. d)   Summary: animal telepathy

The dog experiment shows that animals can also receive telepathic messages from humans.

The "100th monkey" experiment proves that there is group telepathy with animals as well.

The swarm behavior is finally an equivalent to the group behavior with humans.

So far no difference between human telepathy and animal telepathy is recognizable.

IV 3.   Is There "Plant Telepathy"?

IV 3. a)   Threatening and praising

This experiment is widely known by now, but it is still worthwhile to do it yourself.

Experiment 14
Take two identical plants, place them next to each other, and water and fertilize them in exactly the same way. The only difference in handling the two plants is that you praise one and imagine how it thrives, while you berate the other and imagine how you cut it and how it dies.

IV 3. b)   Group consciousness

The following experiment is difficult to perform because not everyone has a lie detector available.

Experiment 15
Cleve Backster, a U.S. Secret Service agent, hooked up a polygraph to his dragon tree in 1966 to measure how long it takes water to travel from the roots to the top of the plant. However, instead of a rash indicating rising humidity in the plant, he found the rash that occurs in people who have been asked an unpleasant question. Backster then tried all sorts of things, which the plant found boring, however, and therefore did not respond. When he had the thought of burning one of its leaves, however, the polygraph recorder struck out – the dragon tree had apparently sensed Backster's thoughts.
The dragon tree even seemed to sympathize with the other plants in the room, as the polygraph connected to it even struck out when Backster hurt other plants near the dragon tree. So it appears that the plants that are in the same place are telepathically connected to each other. This suggests that also in nature the meadows, plant beds, groups of trees, forests etc. are not only an "optical unit" but also a "telepathic network".

IV 3. c)   Summary: plant telepathy

Also with the plants single telepathy as well as group telepathy can be proved.

IV 4. Is There "Stone-Telepathy"?

While the existence of telepathy in humans has made it probable that telepathy can also be found in animals, this was not so obvious in plants to begin with. The question thus arises whether only living beings have telepathy, or whether telepathy even exists in "inanimate nature".

In the search for an answer to this question there is first of all the problem that stones are rather immobile … How should one recognize a reaction?

IV 4. a) Apache tear

Experiment 16
Hold an Apache tear in your hand for one night during sleep.
An apache tear is a smoke obsidian. This is a drop of lava that was spewed from a volcano and fell directly into the sea, where it solidified into a piece of semi-transparent glass.

Smoke obsidian is the most pristine form of stone possible – it is abruptly solidified lava that has not been transformed in any way.

The effect of this stone corresponds to its history: it awakens in a human what this human originally wanted. Therefore, the Apache tear experiment leads one to become aware again of one's original intentions – and also of all the things by which one has repressed these original intentions.

This experiment is not a direct proof of stone telepathy, but it nevertheless shows a stone effect corresponding to the history of the stone in question.

IV 4. b)   Fire opal

Experiment 17
Hold a fire opal in your hand for a long time or carry it in your pocket for a while.
Fire opals, like all opals, are formed in geysers containing silicon. So the formation of opals is based on hot water rising from the earth. The silicon dissolved in this water then settles around the geyser and forms together with oxygen and water water-containing silicon dioxide rocks, thus water-containing quartz. The fire opal receives its red ("fiery") color by the fact that in it additionally iron is stored.

The rising hot water of a geyser is a correspondence to any heat and hot liquids rising or flowing in a human being: They stimulate sexuality, they promote the rising of Kundalini, they sometimes cause nosebleeds, they can cause a sudden violent runny nose, etc.

Here, too, the effect of the stone corresponds to its history of origin.

IV 4. c)   Quartz and rock crystal

Experiment 18
Place some small rock crystals or a large rock crystal at your workplace. Compare the effect if you have quartz at your workplace instead. You can also make a blind experiment out of this by having someone else place either a rock crystal or a quartz in a drawer of your desk or similar in the morning. Then at the end of the day, try to see which stone "accompanied" you.
You can also carry a rock crystal with you or regularly drink water from a glass that has some rock crystals in it.
Rock crystal, like apache tear and like fire opal, is made of silicon dioxide. While apache tear is formed extremely quickly and fire opal is formed gradually, rock crystals are formed extremely slowly. If there are cavities with a silicon dioxide solution in lava flows, simple quartz or rock crystal can be formed from it. A rock crystal can only originate out of this solution, if this solution cools down only by $1°C$ in 100 years. The special thing about a rock crystal is that it has time to establish a perfect inner order because of the slow cooling: Each atom in a rock crystal is connected to every other atom in that crystal, i.e. each rock crystal tip is a single, individual molecule.

A rock crystal is perfect order, perfect integration, and therefore clarity and healing. These four things are also the effect of a rock crystal, which again corresponds to the way the stone was created.

The difference between a rock crystal and a quartz is only the degree of inner order – their substance, however, is identical. Since their effect is different, this difference obviously is caused by this order, which in turn is due to their history of origin.

IV 4. d) Crystal healing

In lithotherapy, the effects of the various stones can be deduced not only from their mode of origin, but also from their crystal form and from their constituents. Their character is therefore not exclusively a correspondence to their history of origin.

IV 4. e) Summary: stone telepathy

For the stones, only their direct effect on man can be called "telepathy". Since thereby the presence of the stones or another form of contact affects humans, this non-physical effect must be counted to the telepathic effects. If people would e.g. eat the crushed stones, this could be a physical effect.

Whether it is a telepathic information, which comes from the stone to the human, or whether this is a telekinetic effect of the stone on the human, is unknown for the time being.

IV 5.   What Happens in the Psyche during Telepathy?

Telepathy is an ability of the subconsciousness, which can be consciously "requested" by the waking consciousness, but which can also be used independently by the subconsciousness, hidden from the waking consciousness.

From this observation it follows that it could be interesting to look more closely at the processes in the psyche during telepathy.

IV 5. a)   Pendulum

In pendulum dowsing, one holds a pendulum in one's hand and lets it swing without consciously doing anything to make it swing.

One uses the arm with which one writes. You hold it bent about the height of the neck in front of you and hold the string of the pendulum with your hand.

In order to use the pendulum, it must be programmed beforehand, so to speak, i.e. one must determine the meanings of the movements.

There are four "distinctive movements" of the pendulum:

- clockwise in a circle

- counterclockwise in a circle

- forward and backward

- from right to left and back

As sensible meanings for the four possible swinging movements the following selection suggests itself:

- yes

- no

- don't know

- unclear/nonsensical/unanswerable question

You can of course think of other meanings, but "yes" and "no" will probably be needed in every version.

Which movements you use for which answers is up to you. It is obvious to use two opposite movements for "yes" and "no" – either the two circle movements or the two

49

line movements. But this can also be handled differently.

One should start with simple questions to the pendulum to get familiar with the process itself: "Am I a man?", "Is today March 2nd?", "Do I live in Germany?", etc.

Then you can move on to asking questions about things that no one in the room knows, but that you can verify. This type of question includes, for example, "How many coins does X have in his wallet?", "How many cars are in the underground parking lot?" or "How many phone calls will I receive today?" By this kind of questions it can be proven that "by pendulum" one can use telepathy (how many coins, how many cars) and also can foresee the future (number of calls).

Now, who is the one who gives the answers during the pendulum? It is certainly not the pendulum itself – but who else?

How do the movements of the pendulum come about? Obviously by the movements of the arm muscles. So there seems to be an instance which is able to control the movements of the arm muscles in such a way that meaningful pendulum movements and thus also meaningful answers result from it. This instance can only be the subconscious, which also contains the entire information of the psyche and which, for example, also controls complex, unconscious muscle movements largely autonomously when walking, talking or knitting.

The pendulum is therefore a "monitor" for the subconsciousness, on which the opinion of the subconsciousness to the posed question is shown by the pendulum movements.

In the house-picture for the consciousness the pendulum "hangs" thus in the office (waking consciousness) – as a monitor on a side table next to the door, which leads into the archive (subconsciousness). The waking consciousness at the office table can, if it wishes, request information from the archive with the help of the pendulum.

Experiment 19
Get a pendulum or make a pendulum (ring on a string or similar) and perform telepathy experiments with it.

IV 5. b)   Finger monitor

Experiment 20
Place your left forearm in front of you on the table. Then place your right hand over your left forearm so that the fingers of your right hand hang freely in the air. Ask your right hand, "Which finger movement should mean 'yes'?" See which of your fingers moves in response. Wait a little while, if necessary, and ask the question again if there is no immediate clear movement. Then ask your remaining three fingers which movement should mean "no," "don't know," and "unclear question."

The automatic movement of the fingers feels a bit strange at first and also looks strange – like a strongly slowed down nervous twitch.

This experiment shows that one can also use one's own fingers as a telepathy monitor. This is e.g. useful in conferences and the like, where it would cause many raised eyebrows if one takes out one's pendulum and uses it.

IV 5. c)   Automatic Writing

Automatic writing is very similar to the finger monitor.

Experiment 21
Take a sheet of paper, place it in front of you on the table, take a pen in your hand that writes as easily as possible, and hold it on the paper. Then ask a question and tell your arm and hand to write an answer. Eventually, your hand will begin to move and scribble something on the paper. At first, these will not be poetic sentences, but probably just strokes that look like "children's scribbles." With practice, however, the subconsciousness learns to link the brain department for writing with the brain department for arm movements and to direct both. After some time, letters, words, sentences and eventually interesting answers to the questions posed will emerge.

One can also use the automatic writing as a telepathy monitor.

IV 5. d) Auto-movement

Now that the arm, hand and finger muscles have become a capable monitor for the subconscious mind, it is natural to extend this monitor further and see what happens.

Experiment 22
First, try telling the arm and hand to make a certain movement. Then wait and see what happens. Next, you can extend the monitor function to the legs. To do this, you sit on a chair and put your right leg over your left leg. Then you simply tell the right leg to "move" and see what happens. Probably the perception of one's own leg moving without one's own conscious impulse takes some getting used to … The same can be done with the other leg. You can also lie on your back, tighten your legs a bit so that your feet come closer to your butt and then ask both legs to move. There are no limits to creativity here. You could also use these leg movements as a monitor – but this is quite impractical for everyday use … Next comes the head's turn. This is a particularly strange experience, because most people locate their personality in their head and can look at the pendulum, the divining rod, the finger monitor and the automatic leg movements still distantly "from above". However, when one's own head automatically moves, nods, turns, circles, etc., then this experiment probably begins to question one's own ideas about one's own psyche: Where and what am I actually when my body, including my head, can move "by itself"? Well, since you probably don't want to stop halfway, you can now sit down on a chair and tell your own body to stand up. The experience of standing up without consciously directing it is indescribable.… Next, you can tell your body to walk a few steps or to grab something. The automatic, i.e. the not consciously controlled movements of the body are completely different from the normal movements – jerky, angular, sudden, they seem awkward, but they are completely purposeful … it has a little bit of a robot …

You can tell your body in this state to do something specific – e.g. to look for something you have misplaced in your own room. You can also tell your body to look for the cure for a disease.

This somewhat strange method can be extremely effective in solving some problems.

IV 5. e)   Search by dream journey

Experiment 23
One can also use dream travel as a telepathic aid. In this case, for example, one places one's own waking consciousness inwardly into an object that one has lost or that someone else has lost. Then you look at your own environment (the environment of the object into which you have transferred your consciousness): Is it light or dark? Warm or cold? Soft or solid? Clean or dusty or muddy? etc. Once one has recognized what the object is in or on, one looks at where the thing is that the object is in or on. Finally, you look at the real (material) place in question to see if the object you are looking for is there.

This kind of dream travel is extremely useful and can be varied for many purposes.

It is also an interesting experience to be the consciousness in a lost door key …

So you can extend your consciousness to objects as well. The experience resembles a dream journey, but the perception contains of course only real elements and no symbols.

IV 5. f)   Dream journey diagnosis

Experiment 24
One can also change with his consciousness into another person. In doing so, one imagines crossing over with one's own consciousness into the body of the other person and looking at him or her from the inside. This looking can be done on the physical level, but also on the level of the life force, i.e. the level of the acupuncture points, the acupuncture meridians, the chakras, the kundalini, etc. The knowledge found in this way should always be checked – e.g. by visiting a doctor.

This experiment feels similar to hypnotizing. This experiment, like hypnosis, shows that one can extend one's consciousness to another person and then see and feel their inner processes.

You may look by this method also for the course of the troubles with the motor of your car.

IV 5. g) PSI experiments

Experiment 25
In the classical PSI experiments 25 cards are used – on five of them each there is a yellow circle, a red cross, three blue water waves, a black square and a green five-pointed star.
Person A picks up a card from the deck face down, focuses on it, and tries to identify what symbol is on the card.
Person B picks up a card and concentrates on it. Person A tries to recognize it.

In these trials, 20% of the answers should be correct – that is, one-fifth, because there are just five symbols to choose from.

It has been shown in these experiments that many test persons at first guessed significantly more cards correctly than would correspond to chance. After a while, however, the number of hits dropped to the statistically expected 20%.

This shows a clear difference between an optical perception and a telepathic perception:

Overview 4: optical and telepathic perception		
Aspect of perception	*Perception*	
	optical	*telepathic*
Motivation	With an optical perception one can look at an object, see it and designate it as often as one likes.	With a telepathic perception one can look at an object, see it and designate it only with sufficiently high motivation.
Process	In optical perception, rays of light that have been reflected from the observed object reach the eye and are then recognized by the brain as this object.	In telepathic perception, the consciousness extends to the object under consideration and recognizes it.
Movement	With the optical perception the information comes to the consciousness.	In telepathic perception the consciousness comes to the information, i.e. to the observed object.
Repetition	The visual perception can become boring, but it still works.	Indirectly, the phenomenon of telepathy fatigue in PSI experiments confirms the model of consciousness expansion.

Telepathic perception can become tiring and does not work anymore.
To show that telepathy exists the postcard experiment is much more convenient.

IV 5. h) Summary: telepathy monitor

The experiments with the pendulum, finger, writing and body movements as telepathy monitors confirm the previous model:

- Telepathy is an ability of the subconscious mind.

- The subconscious can direct the body.

- The subconscious can express the telepathically obtained information by movements of the body.

- The informations send by the subconsciousness into the waking consciousness need a monitor: inner images (dream, dream journey), pendulum, body movements, Tarot cards etc..

The consciousness can extend itself to objects and other people and then recognize their interior as well as their environment.

IV 6.   Summary: telepathy

The previous considerations have shown that telepathy exists in humans, animals, plants and in a maybe slightly different form also in stones. Telepathy is therefore very probably a form of connection between all things that exist.

This "very probably" is only in this statement because one would have to prove also that telepathy works also on water, fire, air, lightnings and the like. But as a first orientation the statement "Everything is connected by telepathy." is well secured by the previous experiments.

With the people, animals and plants a group telepathy can be proven besides. With the stones this is not provable because of their practically non-existent reactivity.

With humans there is intentional telepathy and unintentional, instinct-controlled telepathy. Presumably this is also true for animals.

Between people, telepathy can become very complex, up to the collaborative, telepathically coordinated solution of problems.

Consciousness can be extended to other things and people, which then allows one to perceive the inside of these people and things as well as their surroundings.

The waking consciousness of one person can "turn off" the waking consciousness of another person and then take over the role of the waking consciousness in the other person, i.e., control him by hypnosis.

The subconsciousness can express the telepathically obtained information by movements of the body.

V   What Exactly Happens during Telekinesis?

Now that telepathy has been considered in more detail, the same can be done with telekinesis.

V 1.   What Happens with Paper Wheel Telekinesis?

The paper wheel experiment is a stroke of luck for magic research, because quantitative measurements can be made on it: One can investigate the dependence of the rotation of the paper wheel on various quantities.

V 1. a)   Which resistances must telekinesis overcome?

In the experiment with the paper wheel described above, the telekinetic force has to overcome three resistances: It has to accelerate the mass of the paper wheel, it has to overcome the friction of the paper on the tip of the needle, and it has to prevail against the air resistance.

These three quantities can be calculated quite easily:

1. Telekinesis must overcome the inertia of the stationary paper wheel – the force of the telekinesis must accelerate the mass of the paper wheel. In principle, a constant force, if there are no other factors, should accelerate the spinning top more and more, so that it becomes faster and faster. However, the paper wheel reaches its "standard speed" of about 1 revolution per second quite quickly and then stays at this speed.

The paper used for the paper wheel has a weight of approx. $80g/m^2$. The standard paper wheel with a side length of 4cm has therefore a weight, i.e. a mass of approx. 0.13g.

2. the effect of telekinesis is reduced by the friction of the paper on the tip of the needle. The friction factor between metal (needle tip) and paper is about 0.2, which means that about one fifth of the force of telekinesis is lost due to friction. Since this portion remains constant independent of the speed of the rotation, the rotation of the paper wheel would have to continue to accelerate in spite of this friction – but it doesn't.

3. When the paper wheel rotates, there is also friction of the paper wheel against the air. In contrast to the friction between needle and paper, which always "swallows" about one fifth of the force, the air friction depends on the square of the rotation speed. Thus, air friction becomes four times as great at twice the speed, nine times as great at three times the speed, sixteen times as great at four times the speed, and so on.

The air friction leads to the fact that by a constant force, here telekinesis, a rotation speed is reached, at which the "driving" by the telekinesis and the "braking" by the air resistance become equal. The result is a constant rotation speed.

However, the rotation speed of the paper wheel is so slow that the air resistance plays almost no role.

V 1. b) Paper wheel with airbrakes

Experiment 26
It is possible to attach "airbrakes" to the paper wheel, as in an airplane, in order to increase the air resistance considerably.
Since the "airbrakes" have no effect on the rotational speed of the paper wheel, the effect of the air resistance on the rotational speed of the paper wheel must be very small.

V 1. c) Paper wheel in different sizes

In order to find regularities, it is always helpful to vary a size in an experiment, in order to see which change of the experimental result results from it – in this way one can find quantitative connections like e.g. "double distance = only a quarter of the effect".

Experiment 27

To find out which rules telekinesis follows in the paper wheel experiment, one can cut papers with different side length: 1cm, 2cm, 3cm etc. up to 10cm. Then you can check what rotational speeds these different paper wheels reach.

In the experiments I have done so far together with about 50 people, the paper wheel with the standard side length of 4cm, which I have always used, have always achieved a rotation speed of just a little under 1 revolution per second.

In the series of tests with paper wheel of different sizes, it turned out that I can just about turn the 8cm wheel and that the two very small wheels (1cm, 2cm) cannot be moved at all. Of the six wheels I got to spin (3cm to 8cm), the smallest spun the fastest and the largest spun the slowest.

The measurement of the rotation speeds showed that a wheel, which has a side length twice as large and thus four times the size and mass of another wheel, turned only a quarter as fast as the other one.

The deviations of the measurements from the physical principle "double mass => half effect" were very small – the deviations were clearly below 5%.

This shows that also telekinesis behaves first of all like a normal physical force, whose effect depends linearly on the size of the mass to be moved.

V 1. d) Paper wheel with different masses

Experiment 28

To find out which rules telekinesis follows in the paper wheel experiment, one can cut a paper gyroscope with double mass. To do this, cut a piece of paper of size 4cm·8cm, fold it to size 4cm·4cm, and then fold it into a paper spinning top.

As expected, the paper gyroscope spins half as fast with twice the mass.

V 1. e)   Paper wheel with different mass: narrow

Experiment 29
In this experiment, a paper wheel of size 1.5cm·4cm is used. It requires a little dexterity to place this paper strip, folded as usual, on the tip of the needle.
The paper spinning top spins only slightly faster, although it has only 38% of the mass of the 4cm·4cm "normal" paper wheel. So the shape of the paper gyroscope also plays a role – not only the mass.

V 1. f)   Paper wheel with different mass: cross-shaped

Experiment 30
In this experiment, a square of size 1.5cm·1.5cm is cut from a 4cm·4cm paper spinning top at each corner. This leaves a cross with the strip width of 1cm. If you bend the strips a little down, it is possible to put this paper cross on the tip of the needle.
This paper wheel turns a little faster than the previous one (narrow strip), although it has a larger mass: 56% of the normal paper spinning top. Is this because the greater bending of the arms of the cross makes the whole thing just like a paper wheel of 3cm in diameter?

V 1. g)   Paper wheel with different mass: U-shaped

Experiment 31
In this experiment, on a 1.5cm·4cm strip of paper, 1cm is bent downward at right angles on both sides. This results in a "U": A surface at the top in the middle of 2cm·1.5cm, with a surface of 1cm·1.5cm bent downwards on the outside left and right. This shape is much easier to place on the tip of the needle.
This paper wheel rotates much faster than the "narrow, straight strip", although the "U" has the same mass as the "strip". The faster rotation must therefore be due to the fact that the "U-wheel" has a diameter of only 2cm. Surprisingly, a square paper spinning top with a side length of 2cm cannot be made to rotate at all – it just wobbles a little.

What role does the shape of the wheel you want to move play in telekinesis???

V 1. h)   The posture of the hands towards the paper wheel

Experiment 32

You can hold your hands next to the paper gyroscope in four ways. The arrows indicate the preferred direction of rotation of the spinning top for the respective hand posture.

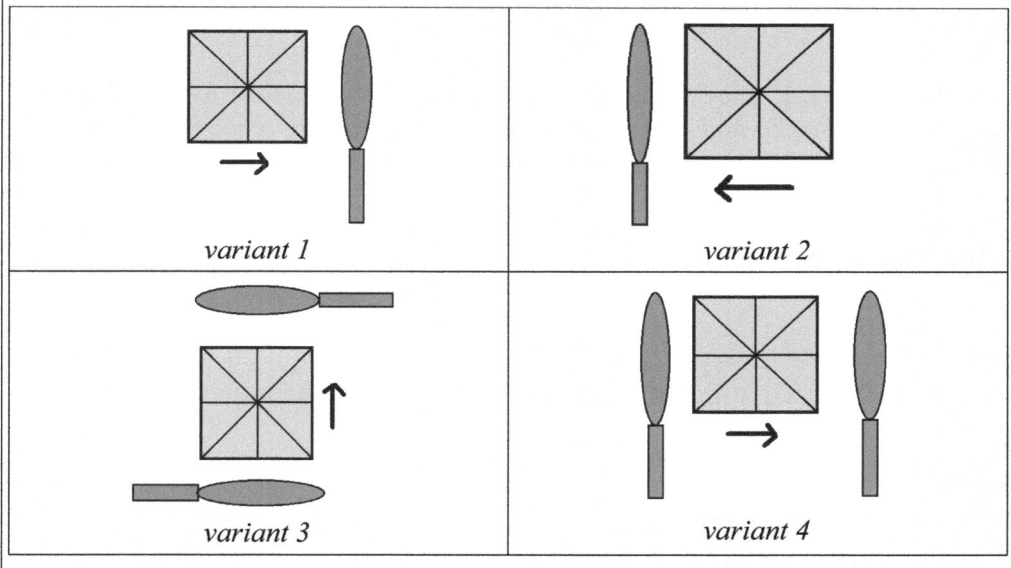

One can observe the tendency that the paper gyroscope moves past the hand in the direction of the fingertips. However, this is by no means a generally valid principle.

V 1. i) The distance of the hands to the paper wheel

Experiment 33
One can also vary the distance of the hands from the paper wheel. With a "normal force", which behaves like the physical forces, the rotation speed would have to decrease with the distance of the hands to the paper wheel.
However, the rotation speed of the 4cm paper wheel remains constant at about 1 revolution/second.
From a distance of the hand to the paper wheel of one to two hand lengths, the effect sometimes occurs that the paper wheel suddenly no longer rotates above a certain distance. Up to this standstill, however, it always turns about the same speed.

So the telekinesis does not behave like an unbundled physical force – like e.g. a magnetic field or like gravity. If telekinesis should follow the same rules as the physical forces, it would have to be a bundled force – like water in a tube, like electrons in a pipe or like the drawbar at a cart.

From a certain distance the contact of the telekinetic force to the paper wheel seems to break off, so to speak.

V 1. j) Turning without the hands next to the paper wheel

Experiment 34
Try to spin the paper spinning top only by your will and imagination.
Again, the constant speed of rotation is found.

V 1. k) Paper wheel with several people

Experiment 35
Turn the paper spinning top in pairs, in threes, in fours … more than six hands are difficult to hold around the paper spinning top at the same time without the need for a larger distance.
Again, the speed of rotation remains constant. The telekinetic forces of the people obviously do not add up and intensify.

V 1. l) Several paper wheels

Experiment 36
Spin several paper gyroscopes at the same time.
Again, the rotation speed remains constant.

This can be explained by the usual laws of nature from physics only if one assumes that telekinesis is not a directed (bundled) force like the water pressure in a pipe or the electrons in a conduit. According to this experiment, telekinesis behaves like an unbundled force – like a magnetic field can attract several iron particles at the same time without this having any influence on the movements of the individual iron particles.

However, the experiment with varying the distance of the hands to the paper wheel has shown that telekinesis must be a bundled force ("water pressure in the pipe"), because the effect of telekinesis is independent of the distance of the hands from the wheel.

The experiment with distance of hands can be explained only by a bundled force ("water pressure in the pipe") and the experiment with the number of paper wheels only by an unbundled force ("magnetic field"). These two results contradict each other quite thoroughly …

From this it follows that telekinesis either follows completely different rules than those of physics, or that there is, as with the wave/particle-duality in physics, a super-ordinate model which resolves this contradiction.

In any case, this contradiction is extremely gratifying, since it contains two results for which a common description can now be sought – such a contradiction can open the gates to new insights in research.

According to the experiments so far, there seems to be something like a "telekinesis constant" (in the following text called „C"), which leads to the fact that the paper wheel with a certain side length (e.g. 4cm) always rotate at the same speed – independent of the number and the distance of the hands as well as of the number of wheels.

One can also determine this telekinesis constant: It causes a paper spinning top, which is made of a square of 4cm edge length (16cm²) and the mass of 0.13g, to rotate with the speed of 1 revolution per second. So we can say:

$$0.13g \cdot C_{Telekinesis} = 1U/sec.$$

From this we get the magnitude of this constant:

$$C_{Telekinesis} = 1/0.13 \ U/sec \cdot g$$

$$C_{Telekinesis} = 7.7 \ U/sec \cdot g$$

However, this constant does not yet include the observation that paper wheels with an edge length of 2cm and less or of 8cm and more do not rotate anymore. For the large paper wheels this could be due to the large mass, but what is the reason for the small paper wheels?

Moreover, this constant does not explain the dependence of the rotation speed on the shape of the paper wheel.

V 1. m)   Paper wheel inside a Farday's cage

Experiment 37
A Faraday's cage is a box made of wire mesh which has the effect that it does not allow electromagnetic forces to pass through. However, placing the paper wheel in a Faraday cage has no effect on the spinning – which rules out the effect of an electromagnetic force.
The other two basic forces can also be ruled out – gravity, because it is so weak and so uniform; and the nuclear force, because it does not act beyond an atomic nucleus.

V 1. n) Candle experiment

One might suppose that the paper top is driven by the heat of the hands – like a Christmas pyramid. However, this is not the case for three reasons:

1. The rotation speed does not depend on the distance of the hands from the paper top, which would have to be the case with a heat-actuated air flow.

2. Tea lights instead of hands don't make the wheel turn.

3. In order to react to heat, the wheel would have to have the shape of a propeller – which is not the case.

Experiment 38
You can place tea lights all around a paper wheel.
The paper wheel does not rotate.

V 1. o) Glass insulator

Experiment 39
Placing the paper wheel under glass seems to effectively stop it from spinning – at least I have not seen anyone "live" who has been able to spin a paper wheel under a glass.
Glass thus seems to be a telekinesis isolator … Or is glass merely such a strong suggestion of isolation that telekinesis does not work anymore?

V 1. p) Summary

The most curious result of the considerations so far is the independence of the telekinetic effect from many factors which one would actually have to assume should have an influence:

- the person performing the telekinesis (different amount of force),

- the number of people involved (more force),

- the number of spinning wheels (more mass),

- the position of the hands (direction of the force),

- the distance of the hands from the paper wheel (magnitude of the distance from the source of the force),

- the airbrakes on the paper gyroscope (reduction of the effect).

Consequently, the telekinetic force does not behave like a physical force.

Now one can see what can be said about this "telekinesis constant".

First of all, this constant appears as a rotational speed constant: The wheel always turns with the same speed.

However, this constant is not absolute, but depends on the mass of the paper wheel. This means that this constant is on the side of the telekinetic transmitter and not on the side of the telekinetic receiver: the telekinetic force has a certain constant magnitude whose visible effect depends on the mass of the moved object.

The object receiving the telekinetic force behaves according to the laws of physics (double mass => half speed). The change from the "telekinetic laws" with their curious constant to the physical laws lies therefore between the telekinetic transmitter (human being) and the telekinetic receiver (moved object) – what is actually self-evident, but in this clarity nevertheless new.

So there is a telekinesis constant. It amounts to 7.7 U/sec·g. Whether this is already the best possible formulation of the telekinesis constant is questionable – but it is a start.

The second, also unexpected finding is the dependence of the rotation speed on the shape of the paper wheel: The straight strip, the U-shaped bent strip and the cross all show a deviation of their rotation speed from the rotation speed of the simple square.

There seem to be at least five influences:

1. a linear dependence of the rotation speed on the mass (double mass = half speed)

2. a minimum mass of approx. 0.03g

3. a maximum mass of approx. 0.52g

4. a dependence on the distribution of the mass (small wheels made of a double layer of paper turn faster than larger paper gyroscopes with the same mass made of a single layer of paper)

5. a still unclear dependence on the shape

Holding the hand next to the paper spinning top during telekinesis is probably only an imagination aid.

V 2.   What Happens during Force Telekinesis?

There is a whole series of telekinesis experiments in which larger masses are moved.

V 2. a)   Smilie experiment

Experiment 40

Smilie

For this experiment you need two persons, a table, a sheet of paper and a pencil or similar.

With the pencil, draw the smilie shown on the left on a sheet of paper and then place the sheet on a table in such a way that you can see it clearly when you stand in front of the table.

Person A stands in front of the table, stretches out both arms to the left and right ("cross posture") and looks at the smilie.

Person B stands behind person A and puts his hands on both of person A's elbows. Then Person B pushes Person A's arms down with all her might. She will most likely not succeed in doing this.

umgedrehtes Smilie

Now the smilie is turned 180°, i.e. upside down.

The experiment is now repeated – person A, who is standing in the "cross posture", now has no chance to keep his arms up …

These two attempts are then repeated with the roles reversed – the "pusher" is now standing in the "cross posture". By changing roles, both can see that there is a difference.

With the smiling smiley you can easily hold your arms horizontally – with the sad smiley this is impossible.

For the explanation of this experiment one does not need telekinesis at first – even if telekinesis could be involved. The upturned corners of the mouth suggest to the subconsciousness "arms shall be raised sideways" – the drooping corners of the mouth suggest to the subconscious „arms shall be drooping".

The subconscious obviously follows in its actions the image on which the waking consciousness concentrates.

This is a context that is also used in hypnosis, advertising, and propaganda. This connection illustrates the nature of the cooperation between the waking consciousness and the subconsciousness.

V 2. b) Dragon claw experiment

Experiment 41
Person A sticks out his right arm with the palm facing upward toward the front. Person B faces person A and also extends his right arm forward, but with the palm facing down. B's hand is resting on A's hand. B tries to push A's hand down. If A is rather weak and B succeeds in pushing down, B puts her hand on A's elbow. Now B raises his right arm in the air and extends his index finger slightly bent like a claw and says: "This is my dragon's claw". Then B touches with her "dragon claw index finger" the spot between A's eyebrows with light pressure. Now B can effortlessly push A's arm down.

Here the arm held up, the word "dragon's claw" and the pressure on the place between the eyebrows ("Third Eye") suggest that B is stronger than A: Person A is the bigger of the two and therefore the dominant person. A is the alpha animal, against whom it is better not to defend oneself.

Again, telekinesis is not yet necessarily needed to explain the result of the experiment – although telekinesis could be involved.

V 2. c)   The "Hepp" experiment

Experiment 42
In this experiment, person A lies down with his belly on the floor and person B lies down with his belly on A's heels and calves. Now A tries to lift B with his legs. I know of only one man who was able to do this – and he got a severe tendon strain … so you should not overdo this experiment, but consider your own constitution. Then you make a second attempt in the same posture. As a preparation for this, A imagines that a white ray of light flows from the top of his head to the soles of his feet and imagines that there is only a small feather pillow on his legs. Then A inwardly says "Hepp!" and lifts B with his legs into the air. Since the legs are bent at the knees in the process, it can happen that B gets so much momentum that he rolls up to A's head or even beyond – so you should make sure there is some space in front of A's head.
If someone is talented for the role of A, two more people (C and D) can lie on top of B, so that now three people are lying on A's lower legs. And Hepp!
Like many other such attempts, the "Hepp" attempt seems to succeed best when several people perform it simultaneously in a larger group. This "group telepathy" seem to stabilize the telekinetic effects of the single persons in this group.
The German word "Hepp!" means "Now!", "Start!", "Go!", "Jump!" etc.. It originates from the French "Allez hopp!", that is used in circus. It's the English "Alley-oop!".

In this experiment, you use your lower legs to lift a weight that your muscles can't actually lift. Moreover, this "impossible lift" feels completely effortless. If you perform this experiment with strength only, it also happens that A lifts himself up into the air with his upper body – simply because the people on his calves are much too heavy. When performing the imagination, on the other hand, A remains relaxed on the floor and B, C and D roll over his back – although, from a purely physical point of view, A should lift himself up into the air.

Since B can not lose mass and also the gravitation cannot be switched off, the effect must start from A. Remarkably, A hardly feels any weight on his lower legs when he lifts B with the imagination "fether-light cushion".

Here telekinesis seems to support the activity of the muscles considerably.

V 2. d)   The chair experiment

Experiment 43

A sits down on a chair and puts his arms besides his body and his hands on his thighs.
   B, C, D, and E put their hands together, make them into two fists, and then extend their two index fingers, which are in contact and next to each other. Then these four people put their "double index fingers" under the two armpits and the two knees of the first person and try to lift him up – which is completely impossible …
 	
   Then these four persons put their hands one above the other on A's head for about one minute – they can also chant "a" together, but this is not absolutely necessary.
   Then the four persons try again to lift A – with a clearly different result …

Again, the four people lifting A do not feel any significant pressure on their fingers. Again, telekinesis seems to support the activity of the muscles.

V 2. e)   The Shaolin experiment

Experiment 44

A places her fist on the table – B and C hold A's fist on the table.
   A now tries to pull his fist away from the table with all his strength – but he has no chance against the four hands of B and C.
 	
   Now the attempt is repeated in a slightly different way: A turns away from the table (his hand is now more or less behind him) and stretches his other arm in front of him so that he can look into his palm. While looking into his palm, he simply walks away from the table and ignores B and C completely – and B and C can't hold him and are pulled away with him …

Again, A does not feel any pressure on his fist when he simply walks away from the table. On the other hand, when he looks at his hand and tries to break away, the pressure of the other hands is very clear.

V 2. f)   Karate

Experiment 45
Experiment 1: Take a stick and hit it on the floor to break it. Then you repeat the experiment, imagining intensely beforehand that the stick will break.
Experiment 2: You place a stick between two walls, between two branch forks or similar and then hit the first stick with a second, stable stick or with a sword or similar to break it.   Then one repeats the experiment and imagines beforehand intensively that the stick breaks.

Experiment 3: Now you try to break the stick not with a second stick, but with the edge of your hand.
   Repeat the attempt and imagine that the stick is only a spider thread and that you do not hit the stick or the spider thread, but that you hit a point 20 cm below the stick/spider thread (the image of the effortlessly reached target). You just ignore the stick while hitting with your hand – like in the Shaolin experiment you ignore the four hands.
   You should not exaggerate in this experiment – your hand should remain intact …

Also with this experiment one does not feel a large pressure on the hand with its successful execution – which would be to be expected actually.

V 2. g)   Summary: telekinetic muscle power amplification

The strength of the muscles can be significantly increased by telekinesis. At the same time, one hardly feels any pressure on the part of the body with which this force is exerted. This striking and repeatedly occurring element of "no pressure" when exerting telekinetic force could possibly be related to the telekinesis constant – both are something constant and effortless and occur in many experiments. However, the exact nature of this possible connection between the pressurelessness and the telekinetic constant is still unclear.

V 3.   What Happens during Firewalk Telekinesis?

Firewalking belongs to the more creative forms of telekinesis, where not only an object is moved or the power of muscles is amplified, but where the normal course of a process is massively changed.

V 3. a)   Firewalk: walking

Experiment 46
Participate in a firewalk and walk barefoot over glowing coals. You may find seminar addresses on the Internet quite easily …

At 850°C, every cutlet burns – why not the soles of your feet? A normal hotplate is only 400°C hot – a modern hotplate is 600°C hot.

V 3. b)   Firewalk: standing

Experiment 47
Just stand in the middle of the ember carpet and wait for a while.

You can also do this without being harmed.

V 3. c)   Firewalk: "The star money"

Experiment 48
Stand in the middle of the ember carpet and take handfuls of embers and throw them up into the air. The embers then fall back down all around you like the stars in the fairy tale "The star money".

V 3. d)   Firewalk: lying down

Experiment 49
Take off your clothes (you may want to keep your underwear on), walk to the center of the ember carpet and lie down on the embers.

The experience is worth it! Afterwards, you'll never think "You can't do that!" again.

V 3. e)   Firewalk: fire breathing

Experiment 50
Put a piece of ember in your mouth and then spit it high into the air like a cherry pit.

V 3. f)   Fire walk: eating embers

Experiment 51
Put a piece of ember in your mouth, chew it well, and swallow it. It's not a culinary relish, but maybe a magical eye-opener …

V 3. g)   Fire walk: Hawai

Experiment 52
These were not yet the most extreme fire experiments – they can be found in Hawai on Mauna Loa: there, the priests of this volcano walk barefoot over glowing lava that has just formed a solid upper layer. This lava is, depending on its composition, between 800°C and 1200°C hot – in the slightly cooled down state thus about 600-1000°C still.

V 3. h)   Summary: fire telekinesis

Walking unharmed over 800°C hot embers contradicts all laws of nature – and even more so lying in these embers.

However, one can burn oneself violently – it is 800° hot charcoal after all.

I looked for rules about what works and what doesn't and tried everything I could think of. However, there don't seem to be any rules – you just can do it.

You don't have to be concentrated, once someone has been pulled along by his girlfriend, also toddlers have run barefoot behind their mother, some women have kept their nylon stockings on …

However, fire seems to have a sense of humor – whenever I thought that I had found a rule, at the next firewalk this rule was disproved by new experiences.

One can say that one suspends the laws of nature temporarily – what one does in a different way also with the "normal telekinesis".

You can also observe, that always those things happen with a firewalk that are best for the person who walks over the glowing coals – whatever this best thing may be.

**With a firewalk everyone bears oneself the whole responsibility
for the what one does.**

V 4. What Happens during Plant Telekinesis?

In the already mentioned plant-experiment "praise and berate" one cannot distinguish for sure whether telepathy or telekinesis works there. Do you intimidate the plant by your own thoughts (telepathy) or do you damage it directly in its substance (telekinesis)?

V 4. a) Green thumb

The same question as to the "praise and berate"-experiment arises also with the "green thumb": Does telepathy or telekinesis work here? First of all, this cannot be decided.

Experiment 53
Some people have the talent to make plants thrive. If you ask them how they do this, you will find everything from affection for the plants to threats of throwing them out onto the compost heap if they don't bloom soon.
It is possible that "green thumb" is an intense variant of "praise and berate."

V 5.   What Happens in other Forms of Telekinesis?

There are some forms of telekinesis that could not be classified in the previous categories. As a rule, the unusual exceptions in research are quite revealing …

V 5. a)   A flying candle

The clearest case of advanced telekinesis I experienced at the beginning of my time as a "magic apprentice", when my magic teacher Axel conjured a demon together with me in his room. A candle, which stood on a holder on the wall, received a violent blow as if from an invisible person, by which the candle flew through the room and then rolled into a corner.

Experiment 54
You can try to repeat this experiment by summoning a demon. Unfortunately, however, this experiment is very imprecise and the results are largely unpredictable …

V 5. b)   Remote thrusts

Another example of advanced telekinesis is the "distant thrusts" that Frater U.D. told me about (he has seen this several times). In such a "long distance thrust" a person makes a thrusting gesture in the direction of another person several meters away, who thereby receives a thrust without any physical contact and possibly falls over. This method is also possible gesture.

Such techniques are found mainly in Far Eastern martial arts and elite military units. These "long distance thrusts" are an intentional variant of the "candle thrust" just reported.

Experiment 55
Unfortunately, this experiment is also difficult to perform, since it first requires qualified training in these martial techniques.

V 5. c)   "Analogy telekinesis"

There is a form of telekinesis in which an analogy is also used. This experiment is attributed to Aleister Crowley – whether this attribution is correct is, as with such things, always uncertain. However, the experiment itself sounds plausible and I have performed and experienced similar things myself.

Experiment 56
A person walks behind another person and imitates their way of walking as closely as possible. This creates an analogy bond between the two persons. By this bond, the second (rear) person can, by a sudden movement of his own, cause the first person to stumble in such a way that he falls down.

This experiment can be attributed to the "steering of people", whereby here more gestures are used than e.g. in remote hypnosis.

V 5. d)   Levitation

Another kind of telekinesis are levitations, i.e. levitating objects or oneself. I have not experienced this myself, but since it is reported from such different cultures as the Indian yogis, Tibetan lamas and Christian saints, the existence of this phenomenon is so probable that it should be considered.

The already mentioned lifting of people only with the index fingers is no levitation, but at least quite similar to levitation.

V 5. e)   Rolling dice without chance

Experiment 57
When playing "ludo" with four of us, especially when my children were present, sometimes a very special high-spirited mood arose, which was something like a "grasped laughing fit with clear direction". In this mood, the wishes for certain numbers were constantly fulfilled – it sometimes happened that someone threw ten "sixes" in a row. After a while it became a bit more difficult, because whenever someone wished for a "two", for example, someone else imagined another point between the two points of the "two", so that it became a "three" … Only the "6" could not be "falsified" by this method.
Is this telekinesis or "steering of chance"?

This "dice steering" can be practiced and used purposefully – so to speak a not provable (and illegal?) falsification.

V 5. f)   The death of a fly

Experiment 58
After I showed my son the paper wheel experiment, he was looking for new applications for telekinesis. Once when a fat fly disturbed him, he waited until it sat down against the wall and then imagined a black circle around it and then drew that circle tighter and tighter. Suddenly the fly fell off the wall dead – at which point my son was quite startled.
There seems to be a variety of uses for telekinesis.

V 5. g)   Summary

There are forms of telekinesis in which larger masses are moved, sometimes quite violently – rather accidentally or also purposefully. However, these forms of telekinesis are not as easy to perform as the paper wheel experiments – they require a special situation, a special talent or a long time of training.

V 6. Telekinesis Consideration

There are four different types of telekinesis, or more precisely, four different contexts in which telekinesis occurs and in which it has different properties.

1. The **"simple telekinesis"**: This is mainly the paper wheel telekinesis. It can be performed at any time and does not require any special practice or even training.

This form of telekinesis has only a small force, which is just sufficient for spinning a paper wheel on a needle point.

What is striking about these experiments is that there is a telekinesis constant: The speed of rotation of the paper wheel depends exclusively on the size and mass of the paper wheel, but not on the number of paper wheels, the number of people involved, the distance of the hands to the paper wheel etc.

2. The **"amplifying telekinesis"**: This includes all experiments, in which one supports the strength of the muscles by concentration and imagination like e.g. in the experiment, in which four people lift another one only with their index fingers.

This form of telekinesis has a great power and amplifies the abilities of the person far beyond what would be possible with the muscles alone.

What is striking about these experiments is that one hardly feels any pressure on the parts of the body with which one exerts this force. One has a feeling of effortlessness.

3. **"Changing telekinesis"**: These are mainly fire walking, fire lying, glow eating, etc.

This form of telekinesis leads to the fact that one becomes insensitive to fire – so to speak "fireproof" like a berserker in the Nordic sagas.

What is striking about these experiments is that there seem to be no generally valid rules for when fire burns the skin and when it does not.

4. **"Extraordinary telekinesis"**: These are such phenomena as distant thrusts, striking an "invisible hand" against a candle, or levitation.

This form of telekinesis has a great power, but occurs in most cases only accidentally and unplanned as a side effect without much practice or special training.

What is striking about these experiments is that there is a large telekinetic effect that works alone, that is, it is not a muscle strength enhancement.

The four conspicuous features of these four kinds of telekinesis could, if they are looked at more closely and combined with each other, possibly give further information about the nature of telekinesis.

The **telekinesis constant** can be explained most simply by the fact that this "weak telekinesis" works from the consciousness on the matter. On the consciousness side a certain constant force is created by the concentration of one or more people, which then acts across the border between consciousness and matter on the paper wheel.

This transition of the force over the consciousness/matter border can also be called an expansion of consciousness.

Why this force is independent of the number of people concentrating on a paper wheel still remains unclear – is there something like a "blurring" at this border, a "partial openness of the border" or something similar?

The **pressurelessness** in "amplifying telekinesis" is one aspect of its effortlessness. Is it possible to move larger masses with this form of telekinesis without any practice because it is thought to be easier to amplify muscular strength by telekinesis?

Again, there seems to be a certain amount of telekinetic power that can be expended effortlessly. At a rough estimate, the increase in strength in these experiments is roughly equivalent to a doubling to tripling of normal muscle strength.

The **effortlessness** in "amplifying telekinesis" gives the appearance of needing the muscles only as a "vessel" for the telekinetic force. The muscles seem to have hardly any function in this form of telekinesis.

The **lack of rules** in firewalking, that is, the lack of any method of walking on fire and any regularity in what one can and cannot do, makes it seem as if one is acting out of a realm of freedom in firewalking – as if one can simply override the laws of nature. There are no rules how to do it, you just do it.

The **"extraordinary telekinesis"**, which is not coupled to muscle power, shows that telekinesis can move larger masses independently under special circumstances. While the other forms of telekinesis can be performed by anyone, this form of telekinesis requires special circumstances or special practice.

The picture of telekinesis, which becomes visible here, makes the processes at the border between consciousness and matter clearer:

1. Telekinesis is the moving or influencing of matter by consciousness (general definition).

2. A small amount of telekinesis seems to be exercisable by the consciousness at any time (paper wheel).
This could correspond to a minor expansion of consciousness.

3. A larger measure of telekinetic power up to about three times the size of normal muscle power becomes possible in physical movements when assisted by concentration and imagination (chair experiment).
It seems to be easier to use telekinesis together with the physical body than to use it outside the body – possibly because telekinesis remains inside the body in this process. This would be plausible in so far as the consciousness is the inside of the body and the body is the outside of the consciousness.

4. With "extraordinary telekinesis" the telekinesis is outside of the physical body. This, unlike the other forms of telekinesis, is not so easily attainable.
This extraordinary telekinesis, which takes place outside the physical body, corresponds in telepathy to astral projection, in which one leaves one's own body with one's entire consciousness – which is much more difficult in contrast to dream journeys, in which one only expands one's perception.

This analogy between telepathy (astral projection) and telekinesis (distant thrusts) suggests to consider these processes at the border between consciousness and matter more systematically. For this one can take the model, which was developed at the beginning of this book, to help and insert these processes into this model – and then see, what results from it.
The six rows of arrows indicate the possible paths that an impulse can take from the consciousness of person A.

Model 10: The forms of telepathy and telekinesis		
Person A		Person B
Consciousness ⇨ ⇨ ⇩ ⇩ ⇩ ⇨	1. ⇨ 2. ⇨⇨⇨⇨⇨⇨⇨⇨⇨⇨ ⇨ 3. ⇨⇨⇨⇨⇨⇨⇨⇨⇨⇨	Consciousness ⇨⇨⇨⇨⇨⇨↘
4. 5. 6. ⇩ ⇩ ⇩ ⇩ ⇩ ⇩		⇩ ⇩ ⇩
⇩ ⇩ ↘⇨⇨⇨⇨ ↘⇨⇨⇨⇨⇨⇨ ⇨ Body	⇨⇨⇨⇨⇨⇨⇨⇨⇨⇨⇨⇨ ⇨	⇨ ⇩ Body

The six paths			
Path	*Process*	*Telepathy*	*Telekinesis*
Path 1	consciousness expands a little into the surrounding space	"feeling" being stared at	oaper wheel
Path 2	consciousness expands into the consciousness of another person	hypnosis	chakra treatment
Path 3	consciousness expands over the consciousness of another into his body	perceiving the body of another from the inside	telekinetic healing
Path 4	consciousness expands into the own body	dream journey	muscle power amplification
Path 5	consciousness expands into the own body and works together with it	---	firewalk
Path 6	consciousness expands into its own body and beyond	---	long-distance thrusts

Paths 5 and 6 do not seem to be used telepathically – the surrounding space can also be reached directly via path 1 and the body of another via path 3.

--- Summary ---

One can describe the differences between the different forms of telepathy and telekinesis by the way of extending the consciousness.

VI   Is There "Telepathic Time Travel"?

So far in this book only events in the present have been considered. A kind of tele-kinesis that works into the past or into the future is also hardly conceivable – a force works where it is at the moment. A telepathic perception of the past or the future, however, would be quite conceivable.

VI 1.   Telepathy in the Present

Telepathy in the present" has already been described extensively – all phenomena reported so far and all proposed experiments refer to present telepathy.

VI 2.   Telepathy in the Past

VI 2. a)   The basic problem of interpretation

Telepathic perception of past things is difficult to interpret:

> - If one cannot prove the perception, one does not know if the perception is true.

> - If one can prove the perception, one does not know whether merely this evidence has been telepathically perceived.
>   This evidence can be previous research that was unknown to the person who "saw the past". It can also be archaeological findings, which have been discovered only after the telepathic perception. However, the problem always remains the same: the perceiver may have simply seen the evidence – the archaeologist's knowledge or the still hidden archaeological find.

After all, these cases are evidence of telepathy – even if one does not know whether it is "telepathy in the present" or "telepathy into the past".

VI 2. b)   Reincarnation

The same problem arises when one wants to investigate whether reincarnation exists. How should one distinguish whether one remembers something directly or whether the information, which one can actually prove these perceptions afterwards, has been taken precisely from this evidence?
After all, if someone can remember in detail the life of a person unknown to him from earlier times, one knows that he can "log in" with his consciousness into the life of a former person.

VI 2. c)   Homeopathy

So another approach is needed to prove "telepathy into the past".
A little trick helps: "Telepathy into the past" is a form of memory, but it is contrast to usually brain-based memory a telepathic memory. If one could prove that there is a

memory which is not bound to a material carrier, one would have proved "telepathy into the past" by this devious route.

Experiment 59
Take homeopathic Silicea globuli and observe the effect.
The effect of rock crystal beads is to promote slow and thorough action. Rock crystal is formed when silica cools very slowly (1° in 100 years), transforming into a single molecule (a rock crystal point).

Experiment 60
Take a Lycopodium globule and observe the effect.
Homeopathic Lycopodium globuli help with the feeling that the great time is already over and you are only living the "movie credits" – Lycopodium was the most widespread plant on earth 300 million years ago, but is now only a small herb at the edge of the forest.

If the effect of homeopathic remedies is not based on the ingredients but on their history (at least in some cases), then the substance in question (here rock crystal and Lycopodium) must have a memory. Since this memory cannot be in chemical form in the plant or in the stone, it must be a "telepathic memory".

By this "telepathy into the past" would be proven.

By this fundamental proof of the "telepathy into the past" it seems now also quite possible that the memory of the life of a former person is actually "telepathy into the past".

In how far the "remembering man" is identical with the "former man", is not yet clarified with it. But at least the possible telepathic coupling of a present human with a human who lived in former times is proved.

VI 2. d)   Information from the past?

In some cases it is difficult to recognize what is actually happening during a process. For example, some years ago I once wanted to write an orchestral piece in the style of Beethoven. I inwardly put myself in Beethoven's place, as if in a family constellation, and composed out of that attitude. The piece actually sounds like part of a Beethoven symphony.

Did I just unconsciously use my memory of Beethoven's music? Or did I have contact with Beethoven's spirit? Or did I connect with the living Beethoven 220 years ago?

Experiment 61
If you want to create a work of art, you can choose the artist in whose style you want to create the work of art before you start. Connect yourself inwardly with him and let him "guide your hand".
The experience is worthwhile – even if it is not entirely clear how it comes about.

VI 2. e) Family constellations

Experiment 62
Tale part in a family constellation.
With family constellation often things are found that happend in the past and which explain the state of things in the present.
With family constellations it is usually not obvious in what way the informations come about – except that the are achieved telepathically.

VI 2. e) Morphogenetic fields

The concept of "morphogenetic fields" is closely related to "telepathy into the past". This concept states that by doing a thing several times, the probability of it being repeated increases.

Or in other words: If an event has happened before, there is a "resonance" from the past to the present that encourages the repetition of that event. This can also be called "memory of the present to the past".

According to this concept, the world as a whole is also shaped by habits.

The experiment of the "100th monkey" is a kind of this assumed effect.

VI 3. Telepathy into the Future

In the case of telepathy into the future, the situation the researcher is faced with is clearly different: The event has not yet taken place and can therefore be grasped exclusively by "telepathy into the future". For a foreseeing to be surely recognizable as such, it must be striking enough.

The first time I tried to look into the future on a New Year's Eve, I saw that I will go to the south of England at the end of June together with a woman with whom I have a relationship, to look at the crop circles with her – at that time I was still single.

The year after that I saw two short but intense encounters with two women on New Year's Eve, which would take place after eight and twelve weeks respectively.

All three events also occurred as predicted. Since then, I have experienced foreseeing the future many times.

A fairly common variant of foreseeing the future is dreaming at night about events that will take place the next day.

Such foreseeing is, of course, only really convincing if you experience it yourself.

Experiment 63
Basically, "future-telepathy" is quite simple: It feels like remembering something you should know – only that you remember the future and not the past. The process is really very much like remembering – the image of the "remembered future" suddenly appears and, if you wait attentively without interfering, gradually becomes clearer.

Experiment 64
It is reported again and again that animals can foresee catastrophes and get to safety in time: in advance of earthquakes, volcanic eruptions, tsunamis and the like.
Of course, it is not to be hoped that you will ever have the opportunity to witness such a flight of animals from a telepathically perceived approaching catastrophe – and to have to ask yourself whether you should not perhaps rather fly along ...

The foreseeing of the future contradicts of course rather strongly the "normal world view". Is everything already fixed, so that one may also already foresee it? Does the human being have a freedom of decision? Or is this subjectively perceived freedom and all "free decisions" just another component of what is already fixed?

These questions will be considered in more detail later in this book.

VI 4. The "Time-Professionals"

There are also professionals of "time telepathy": the Tibetan Tulkus. These are the approximately 1000 lamas, that is, monks who are so advanced that they can, on the one hand, remember their previous life and, on the other hand, predict their next incarnation.

The monks of the monastery to which a deceased tulku belonged then search at the time predicted by the deceased tulku at the place named by him for a child who corresponds to the description of the tulku. Then two rehearsals are conducted: First, the child is presented with some objects, which include a few items that belonged to the tulku, and second, the child is asked basic questions about the Tibetan religion and the various meditations the tulku used in his previous life.

If the child recognizes the items he possessed in his previous incarnation as a tulku, and is also able to correctly answer the monks' questions about the meditations, it is considered proven that the child is indeed the reincarnated tulku. He then returns to the monastery as a child and is trained there, i.e. his knowledge and abilities are reawakened.

By this system, it happens in Tibet from time to time that children are abbots of a monastery – they are reincarnated monks who can remember their previous lives by time telepathy and are therefore, so to speak, several lifetimes old adults in the bodies of children.

VI 5. Summary

There is the possibility to grasp also the past and the future with the help of telepathy – thus telepathy is "time-independent".
Very probably animals also have the ability to perceive at least the near future.

VI Is There a Continuum of Consciousness?

So far only the single telepathic and telekinetic events have been considered. However, the question also arises what the fundamental proof of telepathy and telekinesis means for the general situation:

- Where do telepathy and telekinesis occur?

- Where should one expect it, even if it is not directly provable in the context in question?

- In which events is it of importance?

- What results from the measure of its spreading?

etc.

VI 1. Is Consciousness everywhere?

If one considers the definition "magic is an effect that emanates directly from consciousness" to be sensible, it is of great importance for the study of magic to determine in what beings and things consciousness exists.

1. **I**: First of all, one can actually only say that one has consciousness oneself. That is certain.

2. **people**: By analogy one can assume that all other people also have consciousness.
   It is possible that in meditation one has directly perceived the consciousness of another human being.
   One can also see that other people act as if they had a consciousness: they have a perception and a memory, they want, feel and think … All this is not consciousness itself, but processes in consciousness – but a better approximation to the "cognition of reality" is hardly achievable with this topic either.

3. **animals**:   Whoever has a pet will certainly say that this animal has a consciousness. It has no human language, but it is capable of learning and can express itself and make itself understood.
   Moreover, first of all, there is no difference in principle between humans

and animals: humans are highly developed animals.

One can assume therefore first of all that also animals have a consciousness.

One could argue that only the ability to learn creates consciousness, that fish and lower animals have no consciousness – but the ability to learn is only about the ability to remember previous situations and to discover new behaviors. The ability to learn is therefore about contents and processes in the consciousness – and not about the consciousness itself.

One could also say that the reactions of lower animals are purely chemical-biologically controlled reflexes – but the consciousness is not active instead of physical processes, but together with them. Also in the human being physical processes take place parallel to the processes of consciousness.

Only the contents of consciousness are simpler in the lower animals.

4. **plants**: Plants have a telepathic perception (they react to praise and threats by humans) and they have a memory (as the effect of Lycopodium in homeopathy shows).

Thus they stand, as far as the proof of consciousness is concerned, on a par with the animals.

5. **minerals**: In crystal healing it is shown that the effect of some minerals does not correspond to their ingredients, but to their history – so they have a memory.

In homeopathy, a distinction is made between animal, plant and mineral remedies – that is, "globules" that have been prepared from an animal, plant or mineral source substance. Since all three types of remedies behave in the same way, they should also be essentially the same – i.e. all have a consciousness.

6. **matter**: People can telepathically perceive any kind of substance (e.g. a lost house key) and they can telekinetically move any substance (e.g. a paper wheel).

If one thing affects another, both things must have something in common – e.g. the electric charge, without which no electromagnetic interaction would be possible.

Since telepathy and telekinesis are caused by an expansion or a similar activity of the consciousness, that on which the consciousness acts must also have consciousness – otherwise the consciousness could not act on this thing.

Thus, all things must have consciousness. The contents of this consciousness are various depending on the complexity of the thing concerned.

7. **inside and outside**: From the statement that matter is the "outside of the world" and consciousness is its "inside" it follows that all matter also has a consciousness.

From these considerations three conclusions result:

1st **conclusion**: Everything that has consciousness should be able to perform telepathy and telekinesis (i.e. magic).

2nd **conclusion**: Everything that has consciousness should be able to be influenced by telepathy and telekinesis (i.e. by magic).

3rd **Conclusion**: All things in the world can, according to the possibility, influence each other by telepathy and telekinesis.

VI 2.   What Results from Group Telepathy?

From the conclusion that "all things in the world can possibly affect each other by telepathy and telekinesis" the question arises, what is known about this general possible affecting each other by telepathy and telekinesis.

The starting point is the statement that everything has a consciousness and consequently also the possibility to exercise telekinesis and telepathy.

The question is who or what uses telepathy and telekinesis and what results from it.

There are some examples of group telepathy:

- Group dream travel, which proves telepathic coordination of inner experiences in people;

- the simultaneous inventions of the same thing independently by several people (e.g. the internal combustion engine of the car)

- the phenomenon of the "100th monkey", which proves the telepathically organized group consciousness in animals;

- the lie detector experiment, which proves the group consciousness of plants.

The telepathy connects obviously several individuals to a group – partly also durably or at least over a longer time.

If the consciousnesses of the members of a group are telepathically coupled and coordinated with each other over a longer period of time, this should develop a momentum of its own. The contents of these consciousnesses will at least partially merge into an (unconscious) group consciousness.

This is not a theoretical consideration, since one can also experience this. However, it is difficult to carry out an experiment on this – one can only observe attentively what happens in the groups to which one belongs.

During the time when I was running a health food store together with some others, it happened again and again that at home I suddenly saw inwardly how one of the others in the health food store wrote me a message on a piece of paper. Some hours later in the organic food store I found exactly this message. I almost only "telepathically read along" the messages during their writing, which were emotionally charged – the feelings are, so to speak, the "sufficient postage" on the telepathic letter.

If from the telepathic connections in a group such a telepathic group subconsciousness is formed, it is to be assumed that also these largely unconscious group consciousnesses coordinate themselves again with each other.

In this way, what is called the "collective subconsciousness" arises: a comprehensive web of telepathic connections, which combine from small unities to ever larger units – like the cells, cell associations, organs, etc. in a living being.

The conscious telepathy is obviously only a very small part of the actual telepathy.

The same is true for all perceptions of the human being: most of the perceptions remain unconscious (e.g. one's own weight on the butt while sitting) – only the information important for the conscious coordination of the momentary situation becomes conscious, i.e. enters the waking consciousness.

If all telepathic and physical perceptions would enter into the waking consciousness, this would be completely overcharged and could not fulfill its coordinating task at all.

Probably only a small part of the telepahthic and telekinetic actions actually becomes conscious.

VI 3.   What Results from Telepathic Memory?

The "telepathy memory", which has already been proven by the effect of the homeopathic Lycopodium remedy, has some consequences. The most important of them is that everything that happens in the consciousness is imperishable: there is the possibility to remember everything – even if it is centuries ago.

So there is not only the "individual archive" (individual subconsciousness), but also a "universal archive", sometimes called the "Akashic Chronicle". This archive is the collective subconsciousness.

In meditation, one can also come to a place where one's own soul is located, which has an "archive" of its previous incarnations in this place. These incarnations can be viewed there like film clips. These "films" do not prove reincarnation yet, but they are obviously an interesting "private archive".

If telepathy itself has a memory, also a group consciousness has a memory.

If the group-consciousness can organize itself, it must have a perception, otherwise how should it be able to arrange its contents meaningfully?

If a group consciousness has both a perception and a memory, it should have a similar form of individuality as a human being, an animal, a plant and possibly also a mineral species – perception and memory form the contents of consciousness.

Each group-consciousness is from the group-consciousness of a family up to the group-consciousness of mankind as a whole also a more or less autonomous consciousness.

These group consciousness beings are what are called archetypes, spirits, deities, etc. and that "thing", with which one has to deal with in family constellations.

At the beginning of this book consciousness has been described with the image of a house:

> - the house = deep sleep consciousness (without content)

> - the archive = subconsciousness (all contents of the human being)

> - the office = waking consciousness (the currently needed contents)

> - the desk lamp = ecstasy state (one content)

In this picture, the collective subconscious can be conceived as the city where the house with the archive, the office and the desk lamp of a single person is located. This house is telepathically connected with the other houses – so to speak by telepathic telephone lines. In some cases there are also permanent connections, such as the one between mother and child, which causes the mother to sense when something is wrong with the child.

This city obviously also has a "city archive". So there is a fifth kind of consciousness:

- the city-archive = the collective subconscious = all contents of the city.

VI 4.   What is Life Force?

In connection with telepathy and telekinesis as well as with magic in general the term "life force" often appears. It probably originated from the fact that in magic and in meditation one can often feel an "electric tingling" and a heat that occurs in the various phenomena connected with magic and meditation. Sometimes this life force can also be perceived as a milky white glow with a slight blue shimmer.

The perception alone only says that there is something that one perceives, but not what it is that one perceives.

One perceives thereby nothing physical, thus no matter and also no energy quanta or the like. So it is obvious to assume that one perceives the consciousness directly. In favor of this interpretation speaks that the life force appears as "radiation" of a human being, as the consecration of an object, as a force in a ritual, as the spirit of a dead person, as a deity etc..

All these phenomena called "life force" are forms or contents of consciousness.

Since the human brain has as contents the perceptions of the physical senses, i.e. sight, hearing, smell, taste, touch and temperature sensation, there are also only these qualities in consciousness. So it would be conceivable that the consciousness, if it perceives something directly (by telepathy), expresses this in terms of the physical senses: light, heat, pressure etc..

This "semi-material" appearance of the direct perceptions by the consciousness naturally leads to the question whether it is a "semi-material" substance – just "life force".

One should use "life force" as a term which simply means "direct perceptions by the consciousness". As such, it is quite useful.

Model 10: The interactions		
Person A		Person B
Consciousness	⇔ Life force	Consciousness
⇕		⇕
Body	⇔ Matter/Energy	Body

The life force in man is not a structureless mass, but has the chakras as "organs" and the kundalini as "life force circuit". Both the chakras and the kundalini are therefore first of all structures and dynamics in consciousness.

VI 5. What is Individuality?

In a worldview where the physical world and the collective subconsciousness are equally real and important, what constitutes individuality?

The body is one's outside – consciousness is one's inside.
The individual part of the physical world is the own body – the individual part of the collective subconsciousness is the individual subconsciousness.

The body is composed of the components of the physical world, which one has taken in by eating, drinking and breathing. The structuring of the body is additionally co-determined by the perceptions.
The contents of the consciousness are composed of the perceptions – both from the sense perceptions and from the (partly unconscious) telepathic perceptions. One's own subconsciousness is the individual part of the collective subconscious ness.

The genes (DNA) shape the body – in them it is determined that one is a human being, approximately how tall one will become, to which diseases one tends etc.
In regressions, on dream journeys, in meditations etc. one can see how a life force vortex was formed during the union of one's parents by their orgasms, which is the basis for one's own life force body.
Unfortunately, one cannot carry out an experiment on this life force vortex – one can only see it oneself inwardly. However, there is a phenomenon based on this life force vortex: In women who are in the first two weeks of their pregnancy, one can perceive this life force vortex all around their belly as a force field, warmth, tingling, and the like. After two weeks, this life force vortex has shrunk so much and has become so condensed that it is inside the pregnant woman's belly and can no longer be perceived from the outside.
This life force vortex is a part of the subconsciousness of the father and a part of the subconsciousness of the mother, which combine and form the basis of the subconsciousness of the conceived child. The parents give a part of their share in the collective subconsciousness to the child – this is afterwards the child's share in the collective subconsciousness. However, neither the DNA nor the life force, i.e. one's own share in the collective subconsciousness, is the individuality.

The subconscious consists of all the perceptions and memories that belong to the life of a particular person. The waking consciousness contains some of these contents, the ecstatic consciousness only one of these contents. Consciousness itself can be found in deep sleep and in silent meditation: Consciousness that is aware of itself – without any other content.
This is first of all the best answer to the question about one's own individuality, one's own center, one's own soul, about the seed from which one has emerged.

VI 6. Gods, Spirits & Co.

From the previous considerations it follows that there is a comprehensive network of telepathic and possibly also telekinetic connections between all beings and things. This is the collective subconsciousness.

These connections have a memory of the past and also a "memory" of the future. Perception, memory and foresight are simply three forms of perception in the realm of the collective subconscious: the perception of the present, the past and the future – for telepathy it makes no great difference in which part of time one looks.

This "time-independence" gives permanence to all processes in the collective subconscious, i.e. in the field of telepathy and telekinesis. In the subconsciousness, which one could also call "life force level", all things are ordered by associations, i.e. similar things are stored together.

In this way, "association complexes" of consciousness contents – i.e. symbols – are created. The contents of consciousness organize themselves to more complex forms. Since the contents of the collective subconsciousness are now once in the consciousness, these complex, associative structures in the collective subconsciousness should also possess a consciousness – after all their "carrier substance" is the consciousness.

So there are organic-symbolic units in the collective subconscious, which have formed associatively and which possess a form of consciousness, which very probably also extends from the present into the past and into the future.

The best known unit of consciousness in the collective subconscious is one's own individual subconscious, i.e. the major part of one's own psyche. Every human being and also every animal, every plant, every stone and every matter has such an individual subconsciousness. This form of subconsciousness, i.e. the telepathic perception of the present, the past and the future, is the inside of a body, i.e. a more or less complex structured matter-unit.

However, there are also consciousness units which are not bound to a single matter unit. The simplest of them is the group subconsciousness, which shows itself in group telepathy: group dream journeys, family constellations and the like. A more complex form is the family tradition. The most comprehensive form (in terms of human beings) is the collective subconsciousness of people.

The spirits of the dead are another group of consciousness units in the collective subconscious. In them, the "memory" of the collective subconscious is most evident: the dead are dead, but their memories continue to exist and may contact people in the present and behave like conscious living beings – but like living beings "stuck in the past."

Another group of conscious entities in the collective subconscious are the gods. They have apparently formed from the linking of all the contents of the collective subconscious that belong to a certain theme. The most important of these images is certainly the Mother Goddess.

At least from the point of view of the mankind the deities that belong to a certain topic always exist only after this topic has originated: the grain god originates only with agriculture, the blacksmith god only with forging, the potter god only with pottery etc.. Because of the "timelessness" in the area of the collective subconsciousness, thus in the area of telepathy, it cannot be said, however, which view these gods have on the time and thus also on the time of their emergence.

Such a mother goddess as with the people there is also with the animals: the "Great White Wolf", the "White Elephant", the "White Buffalo Woman" etc.. These animal mother goddesses are often called "white" and "great" because in dreams, dream journeys, meditations and visions they appear about twice as big as a normal animal and have the shape made of a milky white shining mist with a slight blue shimmer. This "life force figure" shows that these mother-goddesses are consciousness beings.

The corresponding deities of the plants are the elves, i.e. the group-consciousness of a plant species.

The deities of the minerals, thus the group-consciousness of the types of rocks could be called "dwarfs".

By the telepathic connection of the individual subconsciousness of a human being to the animal spirits, plant spirits and mineral spirits, the encounter with the power animal, with the power plant and the power stone is created.

The collective subconsciousness of the whole earth including all living beings on it could be called "Gaia".

An interesting phenomenon are astral journeys. In this process, one leaves one's own physical body and can see it lying beneath oneself. In most cases, one perceives oneself as a life force body, a milky white spirit floating above the physical body. Sometimes, however, one experiences oneself only as a "point of consciousness" that can perceive everything around it.

However, the way of perception is usually a little changed during astral travel – one sees things clearly, but as slightly misty shadows. There is also no source of light, but a diffuse light that fills everything. This strange optical perception is probably due to the fact that on an astral projection one perceives oneself and one's surroundings directly from the consciousness and consequently needs no light, even though these direct perceptions are represented by the consciousness as optical impressions.

Astral projection is therefore the complete telepathic perception of one's surroundings – in "normal telepathy" one sees only a small part of one's surroundings. In astral travel, one has increased telepathic perception to "100%".

In magic there are different concepts to explain the magical phenomena:

- The "life force model" describes everything from the way of perception of the processes in magic – just with the help of the "milky white shining mist".

- The "spirit model" describes everything with the help of the conscious entities in the collective subconscious.

- The "collective subconsciousness" model uses the concept of an all-encompassing subconsciousness.

- The "information model" considers the telepathic or telekinetic content sent in the collective subconscious.

- The "psyche model" looks only at the processes in the psyche.

These five models are ultimately the same model, emphasizing only different aspects:

- the collective subconsciousness as a comprehensive "telepathic internet",

- the perceptions in the collective subconsciousness ("life force"),

- the exchanged information (telepathy, telekinesis),

- the entities in the collective subconsciousness (gods, spirits), and

- the share of the psyche in the collective subconsciousness.

In this context, the phenomenon of crop circles is interesting: how do they appear? When one enters a newly formed crop circle, it feels like a transfer of power, like in a powerful ritual, like in an effective healing and similar processes. This suggests a telekinetic origin of the crop circles.

In addition fits among other things also that the grain stalks were often bent at the knots of the stalks – which is physically impossible, since the stalks would break thereby.

But from whom originates this nevertheless very powerful and complex telekinesis? From the collective subconsciousness of the people? Or is it Gaia, that is the earth as a whole?

The grain elf as the originator is rather unlikely, because why should he do that? There the collective subconsciousness of the people or Gaia are more probable – both could have a motivation.

(For more details see my book "Crop Circles for Beginners".)

VI 7. Meditation

VI 7. a) Meditation and subconsciousness

The collective subconsciousness allows another form of meditation. The forms of meditation discussed in the first chapter consisted of the coordination of the waking consciousness with the subconsciousness, with deep sleep consciousness and with ecstasy. This results in the following three basic forms of meditation:

waking consciousness + subconsciousness	= dream journey
waking consciousness + deep sleep consciousness	= stillness meditation
waking consciousness + ecstasy	= one-pointedness

To this is now added another form of meditation, which consists of coordination between the waking consciousness and the collective subconsciousness.

This kind of meditation appears in several forms:

- as telepathy and as astral projection ("100% telepathy"),

- as telekinesis,

- as guidance of coincidence (magic),

- and as invocation (identification with a deity).

The coordination of the waking consciousness with the collective subconsciousness is, so to speak, the "big brother" of the coordination of the waking consciousness with the individual subconsciousness – these two meditation possibilities are, so to speak, the "lesser dream journey" and the "greater dream journey".

Telepathy and telekinesis are generally methods that use the collective subconsciousness, as it consists of these two. Therefore, the meditation form of the "greater dream journey" is magic, that is, the use of telepathy and telekinesis. One of the most important tools in this is invocation, that is, identification with a deity (intense telepathic coupling to a deity).

Thus, there are four basic types of meditation:

waking consciousness + individual subconsciousness   = dream journey

waking consciousness + collective subconsciousness   = magic, invocation

waking consciousness + deep sleep consciousness   = silent meditation

waking consciousness + ecstasy   = one-pointedness

VI 7. b)   Meditation and deep sleep consciousness

The finding that there is a collective subconsciousness of which the individual subconsciousness is a part raises a new question: The individual subconsciousness consists of the contents in the individual "archive". This "archive" is located in the "house" that corresponds to the deep sleep consciousness. This house is the basis for the archive – the deep sleep consciousness is the basis for the subconsciousness.

Therefore, shouldn't there also be a "collective deep sleep consciousness" which is the basis for the collective subconsciousness?

The contents of the collective subconsciousness can be recognized by a dream journey, which arises from the coordination between the waking consciousness and the individual subconsciousness. Consequently, one should be able to reach the "collective deep sleep consciousness" from the silence meditation.

Magic and invocation are two extensions of the dream journey to the collective subconsciousness – therefore, the meditation that is sought here should be achieved by an extension of the stillness meditation.

This is of course not the easiest field of research, since it presupposes first of all that one masters the silence meditation, i.e. can go consciously into the deep sleep state, in which only the consciousness is there, which is conscious of itself.

There are definitely further experiences, which one can experience starting from the silence meditation and which could be experiences in the area of the "collective deep sleep consciousness". These include:

- the direct perception of another consciousness;

- the experience of the one glistening white light that is undivided and the basis of everything;

- an intense inner widening and being fulfilled.

VI 7. c) Meditation and ecstasy

Can there be a "great version" of ecstasy? Most likely still the common ecstasy in sex, in meditation or in mass hysteria …

After all, it must be about a "common unity on the same content of consciousness".

VI 7. d) Meditation and waking consciousness

The same question arises in relation to waking consciousness. Waking consciousness, however, remains limited to the individual human being – however, several people can, for example, make a dream journey together. What is coordinated is the telepathic perception and not the waking consciousness of the involved people.

However, one could consider an intensive conversation between two persons about a topic that interests both of them very much as a "common waking consciousness".

VII   Freedom and Determinism

In telepathy and telekinesis things happen, which should not be possible from a purely physical point of view. Telepathy and telekinesis have no "normal cause" and contradict thereby causality, by which all things are fixed in their course.

It is therefore natural, if one wants to investigate magic, to look at this contradiction more exactly.

VII 1.   What Happens with Telekinesis?

In hypnosis, an effect is exerted on another person. In this process, the waking consciousness of the hypnotized person is "switched off" by the hypnotist and replaced by his own waking consciousness – the hypnotist can direct the hypnotized person from this point on.

In hypnosis, one's own will has been extended to another and the other now does what one oneself wants. The hypnotist has "hijacked" the other person's body, so to speak.

In telekinesis, however, something else happens than in this "hostile takeover" of another body by the consciousness of the hypnotist. In hypnosis, the consciousness telepathically extends itself to another person – since the consciousness is so hard to grasp, this sounds very strange, but to most people, telekinetically spinning a paper wheel is even stranger.

In telekinesis, the consciousness moves another object. The hypnotized person moves with his own muscles, but the paper wheel has no muscles and there is no detectable physical force moving the paper wheel. However, a physical effect without a physical cause is something that should not exist. Therefore this contradiction is an observation, which makes the extension of one's own world view possible.

Why does something move with telekinesis?

The simplest explanation (which does not explain a lot) is, that one expands one's consciousness to the telekinetically moved object and moves ist just as one is able to move one's own body.

VII 2. What Happens with Materializations?

There is a second phenomenon, which stands in an even more glaring contradiction to the purely physical world view: the materialization and the de-materialization. Unfortunately, it is extremely difficult to conduct a focused experiment on this subject. Therefore, instead I report an experience of my own on this topic:

This story about a materialization begins with the fact that I hiked on the Canarian island La Palma and felt the need to wear a necklace again. I asked myself which necklace would be the right one – the pendant would have to reflect my own being and it would have to be made of gold and the pendant should not be too big.

When I got to the beach, I sat down on a rock that was a good three feet high and sometimes had waves crashing against it at the bottom. After I had been sitting there for a while, a high wave came up to me. Then I saw something golden flashing in the spray on the rock between my feet and quickly grabbed it.

It was a golden, artfully twisted chain with a golden Christ as a pendant, who had raised his arms as if in an invocation – but he was not hanging on the cross (which I don't like at all). I didn't know what to say anymore, when I realized that I was holding in my hands exactly the necklace I had wished for shortly before – and that the sea had thrown it to me with a high wave …

When I called my friend a little later, she told me that at the same time I found the necklace, she had spontaneously bought a large mural of Christ in an antique store – and Christ had never been a big topic in our conversations otherwise.

About a year later, I had a major crisis and wondered what to do next. Finally I came to the conclusion that I really had to let go of everything completely, so that what I really am can show itself. At that time I was visiting my girlfriend in Offenburg.

At this decision I was standing at a traffic circle in the middle of a crossroads, where this traffic circle was set up as a crosswalk – you could walk into the middle from all sides and from there to where you wanted to go. This small circular place in the middle of the traffic circle is surrounded by about eight upright stones about the height of a man – a "mini Stonehenge". So I went to one of these stones and squatted down in front of it and took off the gold Christ necklace and the silver dragon necklace, both of which I wore all the time at that time, and put them on the ground in front of the stone and said, "For the one for whom they are intended." Then I looked at them for a moment and left.

About three months later I was on my way from Freiburg to Bonn by railway and stopped at the station in Offenburg for one and a half hours. Something drew me to the "Stonehenge traffic circle" and although I told myself that it was silly and sentimental to think of my two necklaces, I followed the impulse and went there. When I got there, I squatted in front of the stone in front of which I had laid down my two chains. Of course, they were not there anymore – gold and silver do not stay long in a busy public place …

I was a little sad that I no longer had those two chains. When I wanted to get up and go again, I looked again at the foot of the stone – and suddenly my two chains were there again. I can hardly describe how that felt. That was actually not possible – that was really magic or something even greater.

Either the two chains had just materialized again (and "dematerialized" three months earlier) or the two chains had been invisible for three months. The materialization seems more likely, since the place was very clean and was obviously swept regularly and all weeds etc. were removed.

In materialization, not only does an object move without visible external influence, but it disappears without a trace and returns from nowhere. This is in violent contradiction to the conservation laws of physics.

VII 3.   What Happens with Transmissions of Consciousness?

There is another phenomenon that is somewhere between telepathy, hypnosis and telekinesis and also contradicts the usual ideas about consciousness and matter: the transmissions of consciousness.

When someone asks me for advice because of an illness or a psychic problem, I sometimes ask to be allowed to change with my consciousness into the body of the person seeking advice, in order to have a look around there.

For this purpose I imagine to go out of my body with my consciousness and to enter the body of the other person. Usually I start by going through the seven main chakras from top to bottom and look at their condition, as this shows me the general condition of the person seeking advice.

If someone has a specific ailment, I also look at the corresponding organ.

In the meantime I have found out that it is very effective to ask the organ concerned a question aloud and then to let it have my voice, i.e. to go into automatic speech. This is quite fun in a way, because these organs are all quite emotional and speak in a way that I would never speak otherwise. And what the organs say is always quite clear and unmistakable …

This form of "temporary transfer of consciousness" can possibly be seen as a form of telepathic hypnosis.

This form of consciousness transfer can also be used when someone is panicking or is about to have a panic attack or cannot get out of a crying fit. In these cases, almost all of the person's life force is congested in their upper three chakras and the lower three chakras are largely empty.

If one then directs some of the life force back down, slows down the frantically spinning upper chakras and restarts the almost still lower chakras, the panic and crying fit will stop after a while.

Of course, these are all things that you have to try out and experience for yourself to see that they are actually possible and work.

This form of "temporary transfer of consciousness" can also be seen as a form of telepathic hypnosis.

In Tibet, in the "Six Yogas of Naropa", there is a meditation that enables a dying yogi or lama to take his consciousness out of his body (astral projection), to search for the body of a young person who has just died, to revive this body from his own astral body and then to inhabit this young body, i.e. to continue living with the old consciousness in a new body.

This sixth yoga meditation of Naropa, called "Phowa", became popular again a few years ago: In the last scene of the movie "Avatar" the consciousness of Jack Sully is transferred with the help of a ritual from his human body into his new Na'vi body.

This form of "permanent transfer of consciousness" is a very advanced form of hypnosis. The basis for it will quite certainly be the ability of astral projection, i.e. "100% telepathy".

VII 4. How do Matter and Consciousness Differ?

In the attempt to explore magic, one is very often concerned with the relationship between consciousness and matter. It is therefore worthwhile to take a closer look at these two and to consider their similarities and differences.

Similarities

One commonality is that oneself as a human being has a share in both.

A second commonality is that both are a part of the world.

Third, matter can act on matter and consciousness can act on consciousness.

Fourth, matter can act on consciousness and also consciousness can act on matter.

Differences

The clearest difference is that matter is outside and consciousness is inside.

A second difference is that one can "touch" matter, but not consciousness – at least not with the hands.

Thirdly, matter is single and separate from each other (living beings, objects) and tends to disintegrate into single parts (atoms), while consciousness connects with each other and integrates and forms ever larger units.

This third difference has far-reaching consequences:

Since matter consists of many individual parts, which all affect each other, it results from the interaction of the impulses of this multiplicity of these particles that all particles co-determine the behavior of all other particles. The laws of nature result from this interaction.
Matter seems to be essentially a multiplicity.

Consciousness tends either to the connection to a unity or is already from the beginning a unity which differentiates itself by its contents: Gaia consciousness – collective subconsciousness – group subconsciousness – individual subconsciousness.
The consciousness seems to be essentially a unity.

A unity is alone and cannot be limited by anything second in what it is and does – there is nothing besides an all-encompassung unity. Therefore the unity is free.

Matter, on the other hand, fixes itself in its behavior by being a multiplicity (every particle acts on every other and restricts it).

> The laws of nature can be derived from the conservation laws, thus from the fact that this multiplicity in its sum cannot become more and not less.
> Considered in this way, the laws of nature are only an outer limit: nothing can happen that changes the sum of what exists. What all can happen is not determined by this limit.

> A second possibility of the derivation of the laws of nature consists in adding all conceivable possibilities of the behavior. For example, a ray of light could travel in a wide variety of curves. However, to each of these curves there is also its opposite, so that these light beams would extinguish each other. The only way of movement of a light ray, which does not extinguish itself again, is the straight line. Therefore light rays fly straight ahead.
> From this point of view, the laws of nature are only a kind of inertia: Due to the multiplicity of particles involved in each event, a group dynamic is created – a common flow on the path of least resistance.

If now consciousness and matter are two sides of the same world, an interesting effect results:

> The world is determined on its outside (matter) in its behavior, i.e. fixed by its inertia.

> The world is free on its inside in its behavior.

The world is therefore a system which is inert on the outside and therefore apparently fixed, while it is free and mobile on the inside. This makes the world a creative system:

> As long as consciousness does not "interfere", everything runs according to the laws of nature – events flow along according to their inner logic.

> As soon as the consciousness "interferes", however, the course of the events is formed freely – the events then follow the intention of the interfering human being and no longer the inner logic of the things, thus the laws of nature.

This "interfering of the consciousness in the course of events" is called "magic", thus telepathy and telekinesis.

Thus, natural sciences and magic do not contradict each other – natural sciences only describe the inert, habitual behavior of matter, while magic describes the possibilities of creative shaping of this matter.

VII 5. "Ordinary Magic" and "Extraordinary Magic"

The interesting question at this point of the reflexion on magic is now, of course, in what way consciousness can become creative, that is, can perform magic.

From the previous considerations four stages of the development of magic result as well as still another fifth stage, which has however still little contour.

These five stages correspond to the "Middle Pillar", i.e. the five Sephiroth on the Kabbalistic Tree of Life, which describe the relationship between multiplicity ("Malkuth") and unity ("Kether").

VII 5. a) The five levels of magic

Malkuth

First of all, the consciousness seems to be quite passive: one experiences and feels and thinks and remembers and now and then has a clearer intention. This state does not seem to have any great effects yet.

Telepathy is limited to sensing danger (being stared at) and telekinesis is limited (if it occurs at all) to the occasional spinning of paper wheels.

Consciousness merely senses that there might be something else there, but it is limited to occasional experiences that have no major effects.

Yesod

However, when the consciousness begins to systematically explore its own possibilities, its influence on events also grows.

Telepathy becomes the intentional looking and dream journeys, with which one explores his inside. Telekinesis is used to reinforce one's actions (lifting a chair, Shaolin experiment, Hepp experiment, etc.).

The consciousness gets to know its own contents better, understands its own dynamics better and also the division of labor between the four modes of consciousness and it begins to use the abilities of concentration and imagination.

Tiphareth

Next, one will probably discover that there is a "creative center" in one's own consciousness from which all impulses emanate. You can call this center "I", "Self", "Soul", "Essence", "Inner Source" or by many more terms. This center is located in the middle of the chakra system, i.e. in the heart chakra.

Telepathy and telekinesis thus leave the "phase of experimenting to explore one's own possibilities". Telepathy and telekinesis become instead the assistants of this center, the "eyes" and "hands" of this center.

The consciousness now begins to shape its situation consciously from its center with the help of its body and with the help of its magic.

Da'ath

This is followed at some point by the discovery of the collective subconsciousness. The center of consciousness experiences itself as part of this continuum of consciousness that encompasses all consciousnesses, that is, the inside of all things.

By the expansion of the consciousness to the collective subconsciousness, thus by the awake conscious perception of the contents of the collective subconsciousness, the possibilities of telepathy and telekinesis also grow. Both are now exercised not only out of one's own individual realm, but out of the collective realm.

The consciousness now begins to act as part of the whole – e.g. by identifying with a deity. Thus, "human magic" expands into "deity magic": "ordinary magic" becomes "extraordinary magic," sorcery becomes miracles.

Kether

The last step is the experience of the Unity itself, that is, the experience of the One Consciousness, in which the contents of the collective consciousness are located – just as the contents of the individual subconsciousness are located in the deep sleep consciousness of the individual human being. Just as the deep sleep consciousness of the individual human being is silent and "empty", i.e. free of contents, this "universal deep sleep consciousness" is also silent, empty, free of contents, undivided, one and all encompassing.

This consciousness can be experienced in meditation. A first impression of this consciousness can be gained by dream journeys to Kether.

What does the magic of Kether look like? It should be effortless and comprehensive – but when one has arrived in Kether, one no longer has any desires that one would want to realize by "Kether magic" …

VII 5. b) The types of perception in magic

In each of these five realms, and to some extent at the transitions between them, there is a different form of perception – by which one can distinguish, among other things, in which realm one is currently perceiving something.

The outer perception
(Malkuth)

The outer perception happens with the eyes. One sees things that emit light or that are illuminated by light when this light reaches the eye. The optical impression in the brain represents the external form of what is seen.

The area perceived in this way is the external material world.

The transition to the inner perception

The transition to inner perception is, for example, the beginning of a dream journey in which one steps through an imagined door or inwardly addresses a deity. Also the beginning of a daydream is such a transition – although not a conscious one. Likewise, the beginning of imaginations during a ritual is such a transition, or the laying of hands on a tree when one wants to converse with it. Looking into a crystal ball or a mirror is also one of these transitions, as is shifting one's consciousness into the body of another person when one wants to see what is wrong with him or when one wants to heal him. Furthermore, the conscious exercise of telepathy and telekinesis as well as hypnosis also belong to these transitions. The transition from the waking consciousness to the subconsciousness shows a great variety …

From the point of view of perception as well as from the point of view of imagination, first impressions, lines, symbols, color impressions arise during this transition, which then gradually become clearer.

The perception in the psyche
(Yesod)

The perception or imagination in the subconscious (= dream consciousness, life force body, astral body) consists of only slightly colored black and white pictures. The scenery is everywhere filled with a diffuse light, which has no recognizable light source. Things move, the scenes sometimes change abruptly, you yourself are part of the action.

This area corresponds to the perception that is artificially evoked by hashish, among other things – however, this state may be much easier (and moreover legal) achieved by a dream journey.

The area perceived in this way is the individual subconscious.

The transition to the soul

At this transition, things partly start to glow from within, they become colorful for the most part, they have unnaturally sharp contours and they constantly change into new forms, these transformations looking like clay being deformed more and more – they are flowing transformations.

This kind of perception is typical for LSD and for quite deep meditations – it is often found depicted in psychedelic art. Anesthetic injections (e.g. at the dentist) can sometimes have this effect as well – it looks something like the things you look at for a while seem to form bubbles and start "bubbling".

The visions of Dr. Strange in the MCU-film "Dr. Strange" are partly a good illustration of this kind of perceptions.

The perception in the soul realm
(Tiphareth)

The images are usually still images (they do not move or change). Occasionally they are symbols. They are colored and they glow from within. These images have a deep meaning that you can feel, even if you don't necessarily understand it right away.

The realm perceived in this way is one's deep sleep consciousness, which is the consciousness of one's soul.

The Transition to the Deity Realm

Things begin to glow more and they begin to become transparent. This means that you can see everything from any place. Intense feelings can occur here, because the boundaries begin to dissolve – which sometimes manifests itself in the vision of a bottomless abyss into which one is supposed to jump.

The perception in the deity realm
(Da'ath)

Here contours in the light are found. This area is a continuum, i.e. there are no boundaries. Here one can only define oneself by one's own quality, but not by a delimitation – one is part of an endless continuum.

The area perceived in this way is the collective subconsciousness. The images in this realm are the deities.

The transition to unity

There are two important experiences at this transition: One is home, a connectedness with everything (Tree of Life: "Binah"), a rediscovery of one's "family".

The drug "ecstasy" is an attempt to bring the human being in contact with this realm in a chemical way.

The other experience is the "light storm", which is an unrestricted self-expression (Tree of Life: "Chokmah").

The perception in the Unity Realm
(Kether)

The perception of this realm is glistening white light or shining blackness – which is a difference only in words. This area is the oneness, unstructured, boundless … and fulfilling …

The "home", the "storm of light" and the "oneness" can be experienced among other things in dream journeys to the plant "sage".

The area perceived in this way is the unity of consciousness, so to speak the "collective deep sleep consciousness".

VII 5. c)   The Middle Pillar and the forms of consciousness

On the Middle Pillar, the three forms of consciousness, waking consciousness, subconsciousness and deep sleep, are found once as an individual trinity and once as a collective trinity. The consciousness form of ecstasy does not appear in this diagram.

Tree of Life	Consciousness	
Sephiroth	individual	collective
Kether		greater deep sleep consciousness
Da'ath		greater subconscious
Tiphareth	lesser deep sleep consciousness	greater waking consciousness
Yesod	lesser subconsciousness	
Malkuth	lesser waking consciousness	

Overview 6: Middle Pillar and Forms of Consciousness

VII 5. c)   Is there a "magic power"?

These considerations show that the concept that telepathy and telekinesis are based on some kind of "force" is not true. Magic is based on the "creativity of consciousness".

119

VIII Analogies

Analogies play a great role in magic. In order to be able to judge their nature and assess their significance, they must first be proven.

VIII 1. The Proof of Analogies

Fortunately, analogies can be proven quite easily and in many ways.

VIII 1. a) Astrology

Experiment 65
Observe for one year what is different on full moons than on other days.
Probably you will find more tensions, chaos, conflicts and the like. This powerful tension can be used for transformations by clear decisions.

Experiment 66
Calculate and interpret the horoscopes of three different people and compare these horoscopes with the character of the people for whom they are calculated and observe the great differences in character described by the horoscopes.
It can be determined quite quickly that horoscopes "work" – even though it will probably take you a little longer to get used to the fact that they work.

Astrology can be used to predict events or qualities on certain days.

The simplest form of prediction is simply that it is already known what character the people will have who will be born in the future – as soon as one knows the place and date of birth, one can also describe the character.

From the fact that one can say now already, which character a person will have, who will be born on 1.1. 2304 at 12.00 o'clock at noon in Berlin, results that the future is already fixed in relation the astrology. One does not know which skin color the person concerned will have and also not which language he will speak, but one knows which character he will have.

Astrological predictions show two interesting phenomena:

- They do not specify an event in a causal way, but from its quality.

- They define an event in a timeless way, since one can always calculate the quality for any place and time on Earth – no matter if it is in the present, in the past or in the future.

Astrology stands from its quality thus between the determinacy of the material world and the freedom of the consciousness.

One can therefore assume that the analogies are located at the border between consciousness and matter, between inside and outside – and thus in the realm, whence magic originates.

VIII 1. b)   Omens and oracles

Experiment 68

Watch for special events that strike you and see what they tell you.

Omen interpretation requires a little practice – however, there are omens that can no longer be misunderstood. The following is the clearest omen I have experienced so far:

I have been friends with a couple who are both sculptors. I would have liked to have had closer contact with the woman.

One day I was standing by a work of art that they had both created together. Then the question came up in me what would actually happen if I would simply do what I felt like doing and not constantly take their relationship into consideration.

Immediately after I became aware of this possibility of action and this question, I felt the urge to go to the ditch that ran 10m away from the artwork. When I looked down the 4m into this ditch, through which a brook from the forest flowed down into the valley of the Rhine, I saw three arrows stuck in the ground down by the brook.

I went down into the ditch and took a closer look at these arrows. On the side of the stream facing the work of art, two arrows of the same kind were stuck in the ground next to each other; on the other side, a different-looking arrow was stuck in the ground, its tip missing and its notch half broken off.

The interpretation was not difficult: the man was Sagittarius by the sign of the zodiac, i.e. he symbolically gave me the answer with the arrows – so the omen was possibly influenced by the man's point of view.

Two of the same arrows are a pair on the artwork side of the stream – the two sculptores. The third arrow is separated from this pair by the brook – me. It is also "neutered" by the broken notch and missing tip.

This didn't look like much was going to happen between me and the woman ….

Experiment 69
Use the Tarot, the I Ching, the Ifa Oracle or any other oracle for a while and see how reliable it is.

The omens and the oracles make the same kind of statements as astrology: they describe qualities and connections.

122

VIII 1. c)   Analogy magic

One can use the analogy principle not only as in astrology, in the omens and in the oracles as an aid to knowledge, but also as an aid to action in magic.

Experiment 70
For example, one can make a talisman for a specific purpose – e.g., a square plate made of pewter with the Jupiter symbol (♃) engraved on one side and "prosperity" written on the other. This talisman is then still consecrated by a ritual or meditation with the quality of Jupiter, i.e. connected with the planet Jupiter or put in analogy with him.

Experiment 71
If you are on the road and have no way to get the appropriate homeopathic remedy for an illness you have contracted, you can also simply write the name and potency of the remedy on a piece of paper, dip the piece of paper in a glass of water, and then drink that water.
Here the slip of paper with the name of the remedy is a very simple analogy to the remedy itself – the "slip of paper water" works just as well as the remedy itself.

Experiment 72
The most famous analogy magic is probably the voodoo doll: Everything that is inflicted on the puppet also happens to the one that this puppet represents.

An important point in all analogy magic is that the effect depends on the one hand on the exactness of the analogy used, but on the other hand also on the intensity of the concentration on the desired target.

VIII 1. d)   Sender and receiver

Is there a "sender" and a "receiver" in analogy?

In astrology, one would first tend to think of the planets as the "sender" – but this is merely because the planets are so large and their movements are already fixed – they cannot be a "receiver" of the tiny and very divers human actions.

However, what about the arrow omen just described? The arrows were shot into the ditch before I asked my question … and they gave a perfect answer … Here there is no "sender" and no "receiver", but only a matching of two events.

The processes in which analogies are involved are apparently "timeless" and therefore are not causal relationships that have a cause and an effect – cause and effect is a consideration along the timeline.

This fits well with the assumption that analogies are located at the transition from consciousness to matter.

VIII 2.   The Universal Effect of Analogies

It is possible to make horoscopes not only for human beings, but also for animals, plants, workpieces, enterprises, states, etc. Horoscopes can be made – they work. This shows that astrology is effective at all times and in relation to everything. There is therefore a universal analogy structure, and consequently also something like an "all-encompassing astrological rhythm", in which all things vibrate.

Also omens and oracles work in every situation. The same applies also to analogy magic.

If matter is the outside of the world and consciousness is the inside of the world, then there is a transition from inside to outside everywhere in the world.

If analogies are located at this transition and this transition is everywhere, then these analogies should also be located everywhere – as it is clearly visible by astrology.

VIII 3. Analogies in Consciousness and Matter

If matter is the outside of the world and consciousness is the inside of the world, then there should be elements that are found in both the inside and the outside. Or in other words: If physics describes the world correctly and if magic describes the world correctly, there should be corresponding elements in both descriptions.

Physics and magic look at the world from different perspectives:

- Physics and generally natural sciences regard temporal processes, thus the connections between a cause and the effect originated by it.

- Magic looks at the simultaneity of two things (astrology) or the qualitative connection between two things (question and omen).

Physics and magic thus look at the world from two different perspectives: physics looks at temporal processes, magic looks at connections in the present.

Despite this different perspective, both look at the same world and should therefore see the same. By the different perspective the things should look different, but have the same structure, i.e. the world shpuld be clearly recognizable as the same world.

VIII 3. a) The angles

The angles as the smallest structural element are found in astrology as the aspects between the planets, whose quality is exactly defined. So one can see if these angles with their qualities found in astrology are also found in the natural sciences.

There are three basic forces: the gravitation, the electromagnetic force and the so-called color force.

The gravitation pulls all things together - one can call it therefore "unipolar". The "unipolar" angle in astrology is the **conjunction** (0° angle), which unites two things into one – which corresponds to the effect of gravitation.

The electromagnetic force is "bipolar" (+ and –) and becomes neutral to the outside by the combination of both poles. The "bipolar" angle appears in astrology as the **opposition** (180°), which, like the electromagnetic wave (light), is an oscillation, that is, the constant change between two poles.

The color force is "three-polar" ("yellow" and "red" and "blue"). It holds together, for example, the three quarks in a proton – if you want to take one of these quarks out of the proton, you have to expend so much energy that a new proton, i.e. a new group of three quarks is created out of this energy … so you cannot separate these three quarks. The "three-polar" aspect in astrology is the **trine** (120° angle) that holds together two planets that are zodiac signs with the same element (fire, water, air, earth).

There are some more angles to be found that have the same quality in physics and magic/astrology:

The astrological **square** (90°) separates two planets in the way a tent pole separates the floor tarp from the ceiling tarp: the separation creates a space. This phenomenon can be observed, for example, in an electromagnetic wave whose magnetic wave is always at right angles (90°) to the electric wave.

The astrological **sextile** (60°) arranges equal elements to a group. This can be found in many places in nature: the water molecules in the snowflake form structures with 60° angles, the protons and neutrons ("equal-sized spheres") lie in the atomic nuclei at 60° angles to each other, around one planet six moons can orbit on the same orbit at a distance of 60° from each other, etc.

So the qualities of the angles in astrology and in natural sciences coincide.

These angles are also found with the same quality in stone healing in the various crystal lattices based on the angles between the ions in the crystal lattice.

(A detailed desciption and a lot of examples may be found in my book "The Synthesis of Physics and Magic".)

VIII 3. b)   The Kabbalistic Tree of Life

The Tree of Life is basically a very simple structure. Its basic principle is unity as the starting point and multiplicity as the result, with a developmental step or differentiation in between. The middle step of this "three-step" is differentiated again into three steps and these three steps are differentiated again into three steps each, i.e. into nine middle steps. In this way, a differentiated development structure results.

The Tree of Life is a very helpful foundation and map both in meditation and in magic. The already mentioned "Middle Pillar" consists of the five Middle Spheres ("Sephiroth") on this Tree of Life. The Middle Pillar is the second step of differentiation, where the step between Unity and Multiplicity is broken down into three steps – in the diagram below "Differentiation II".

Overview 7: the Kabbalistic Tree of Life					
Differentiation			*Sephiroth*	*Planet*	*Tree of Life*
I	*II*	*III*			
1.	1.	1.	Kether	Pluto	
		2.	Chokmah	Neptune	
	2.	3.	Binah	Uranus	
		D	Da'ath	Saturn	
		4.	Chesed	Jupiter	
2.	3.	5.	Geburah	Mars	
		6.	Tiphareth	Sun	
		7.	Netzach	Venus	
	4.	8.	Hod	Merkury	
		9.	Yesod	Moon	
3.	5.	10.	Malkuth	Earth	

Since this structure has been derived in a simple, logical way, it can be found in everything – from the structure of a vacuum cleaner to the classical ballet and the chakra system to the constitution of a state (see my three books "Blüten des Lebensbaumes" I - III).

The superstring theory used by physicists today is a very complex model. To describe it, a mathematical model is needed, which uses not only the three space dimensions and the one time dimension familiar from everyday life, but seven additional space dimensions, which, however, become visible only in areas far smaller than an electron. One of these seven additional dimensions has the property that it "wraps up" the other ten dimensions, thus summarizes them.

This eleven-dimensional mathematical model corresponds exactly to the Kabbalistic tree of life:

- The topmost of these eleven spheres (Kether) corresponds to the time dimension.

- The three spheres below it (Chokmah, Binah, Da'ath) correspond to the three "normal" space dimensions.

- The six following spheres (Chesed, Geburah, Tiphareth, Netzach, Hod, Yesod) correspond to the six "hidden" space dimensions.

- The lowest sphere (Malkuth) corresponds to the "summarizing" dimension.

The Tree of Life is the most differentiated analogy structure known so far. It consists of 40 elements: the 11 spheres ("Sephiroth"), the 22 paths between them, the 3 triangles, the 4 transitions between the five spheres on the Middle Pillar, and so on.

It can be found everywhere – even in the "heart of physics", as which the superstring theory can be called a little poetically.

VIII 3. c)   The zodiac

The central element of astrology is the zodiac. It actually has a very striking structure – twelve equal parts forming a circle, which are sharply delimited from each other and which, moreover, have properties that can be described with the help of aspects (angles): each sign is identical with itself (conjunction), opposite signs are complementary opposites (opposition), signs standing in a triangle have the same element (trine), signs standing in a square have the same dynamics (square), signs standing in a hexagon form a common group (sextile), and so on.

The central element of the superstring theory, with which the whole of physics is described today, is the Heisenberg spin chain, usually called "superstring". It has a actually very conspicuous structure – twelve equal parts which form a circle, which are sharply separated from each other and which have, besides, properties which can be described with the help of the angles (aspects): This Heisenberg spin chain is like a string stretched in a circle, which vibrates – six of of the twelve sections vibrate downwards, the other six vibrate upwards (the two groups vibrate alternately upwards and downwards), the twelve boundary points between them are always at rest. The two groups of six correspond to the two hexagons on the zodiac – the fire/air signs and the water/earth signs.

Thus, the basic "building block" in astrology and in physics also has exactly the same structure.

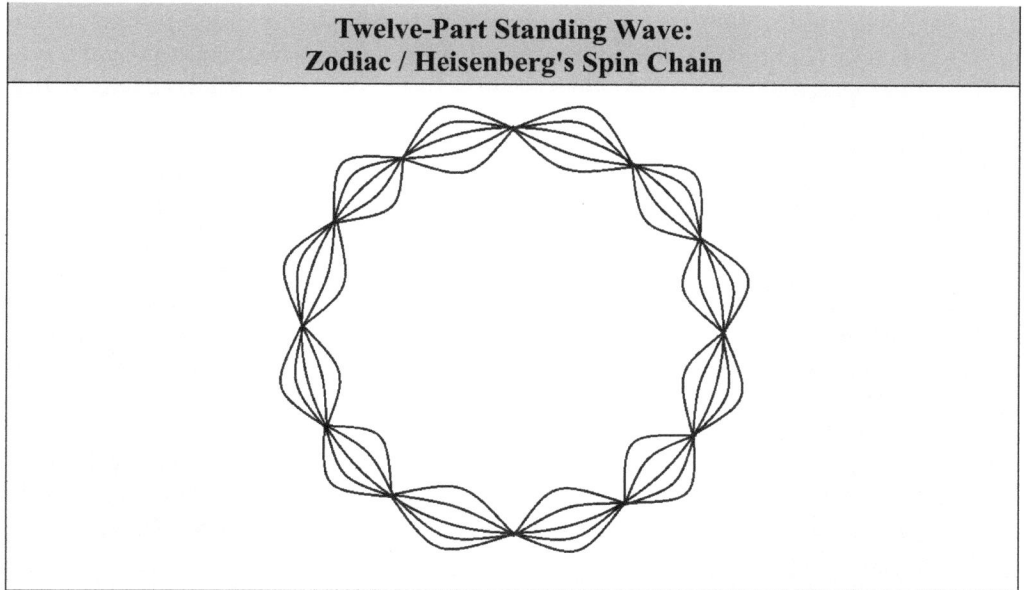

Twelve-Part Standing Wave:
Zodiac / Heisenberg's Spin Chain

The zodiac as a building plan of the physical world appears a second time very clearly: The world is built up of four kinds of particles: the up-quark, the down-quark, the electron and the neutrino. These four particles appear in three different sizes.

This structure corresponds obviously to the zodiac in which there are four elements which appear in three dynamics.

The natural scientists and the magicians/astrologers describe the world with different words, but with exactly the same structure.

VIII 3. d)   The chakra system

The structure of the chakra system is quite different from the organs in a living being. Interestingly, however, the structure of the chakras, that is, the organs of the life-force body of a human being, completely coincides with the structures around a sun.

> The center is the radiant sun.
> It corresponds to the radiant heart chakra.

129

Around the sun there is an area which is completely characterized by the photons (light) and the ions (electrically charged particles) emitted by the sun. In this area all matter ("stardust") has been blown away to the outside by this "solar wind".

This area around the sun, which is completely shaped by the sun, corresponds to the unrestricted physical self-expression of the solar plexus and the unrestricted social self-expression of the throat chakra.

The solar wind pushes all small-grained matter ("stardust") in its surrounding space outward and away from the sun on all sides like a snow pusher. This forms a kind of wall in front of the solar wind, consisting of the stardust and ions emitted by the sun. It is called the "shock front." The total mass of this "envelope" is approximately equal to the mass of the Earth, but it consists only of finely spread dust.

This envelope around the area directly around the sun, which is shaped by the solar wind, corresponds to the two form chakras: The hara gives man a firm inner support and the third eye gives man an orientation in the whole surrounding space.

The shock front gradually moves further and further outward away from the sun, since the solar wind constantly blows against this shock front from within and constantly gives it new thrust. Thus the area shaped by the solar wind becomes ever larger around the sun. This expanding shock front, which is a spherical shell of stardust and solar ions, moves through the stardust in space like a ship in water. This creates a "bow wave" of stardust in front of the shock front.

This "bow wave" corresponds to the two outer chakras, which, like the bow wave, make contact with the environment: The root chakra is the physical contact and the crown chakra is the spiritual contact.

These three spaces around the sun (solar wind space, shock front, bow wave) correspond to the qualities of the three pairs of chakras. The sun itself corresponds to the heart chakra.

But the analogy between the solar system and the chakra system does not end there:

The sun contains ions, electrically charged particles. When an electric charge moves (as in the case of the sun by its rotation), a magnetic field is created. The magnetic field is always at right angles to the direction of motion of the electric charge. With a rotating sphere this results in two rays emerging from the two poles of the star, planet or galaxy. They are two beams because there are both positively and negatively charged ions and the magnetic fields created by their motion point in opposite directions. This is also how the

130

magnetic north pole and the magnetic south pole of the Earth are created, which allow the use of a compass. These two magnetic beams coming out of the poles of the sun are called "jets".

These two "jets" are found in the life force body as the path of the Kundalini, which rises from the lower chakra to the highest chakra. This path ("life force channel") is called "sushumna" in yoga – it leads from the heart chakra ("sun chakra") down to the root chakra and up to the crown chakra.

At the points where this "jet" flies from the two poles of the sun through the three areas, vortices are formed.

These "vortices" at the points where the two jets fly through the three areas of the sun's circumference correspond to the three chakras above the heart chakra and below the heart chakra. The vortex at the jets corresponds to the circular motion of the chakras.

The magnetic jets, in turn, act on the ions around them, accelerating them outward away from the sun. Since these ions usually already have a motion of their own, they do not fly away outward in a straight line in the jets themselves, but assume an outwardly moving spiral path around the jet. In doing so, the negatively charged ions rotate in a spiral whose direction of rotation is opposite to the spiral of the positively charged ions.

In yoga, these two spirals are found as the two secondary "life force channels" Ida and Pingala. Since these spiral movements can only be reproduced two-dimensionally on the drawings (in the yoga scriptures), they appear as two symmetrical serpentine lines (as also on the Hermes staff). In Ida and Pingala the inner female-image and the inner male-image are found, which corresponds to the opposite charge of the ions in the two spirals. In the central "life force channel", which is called "Sushumna" in yoga, is the gender-independent self-image of the human being.

In the sun, there is a convection current: in the center, matter is heated by the nuclear fusion that takes place there, rises upward like the water jet of a fountain, spreads out on the surface like the fountain of a waterspout fountain, cools down there, and then sinks down again like the drops of a fountain.

In the life force body, there is a convection current: from the root chakra, the life force rises upward like the water jet of a fountain ("awakened Kundalini"), spreads out like the fountain of a fountain on the surface (surface of the aura), and then sinks back down to the root chakra like the drops of a fountain.

The similarity between the two systems becomes clearer when represented graphically:

Overview 8: The solar system and the chakra system.

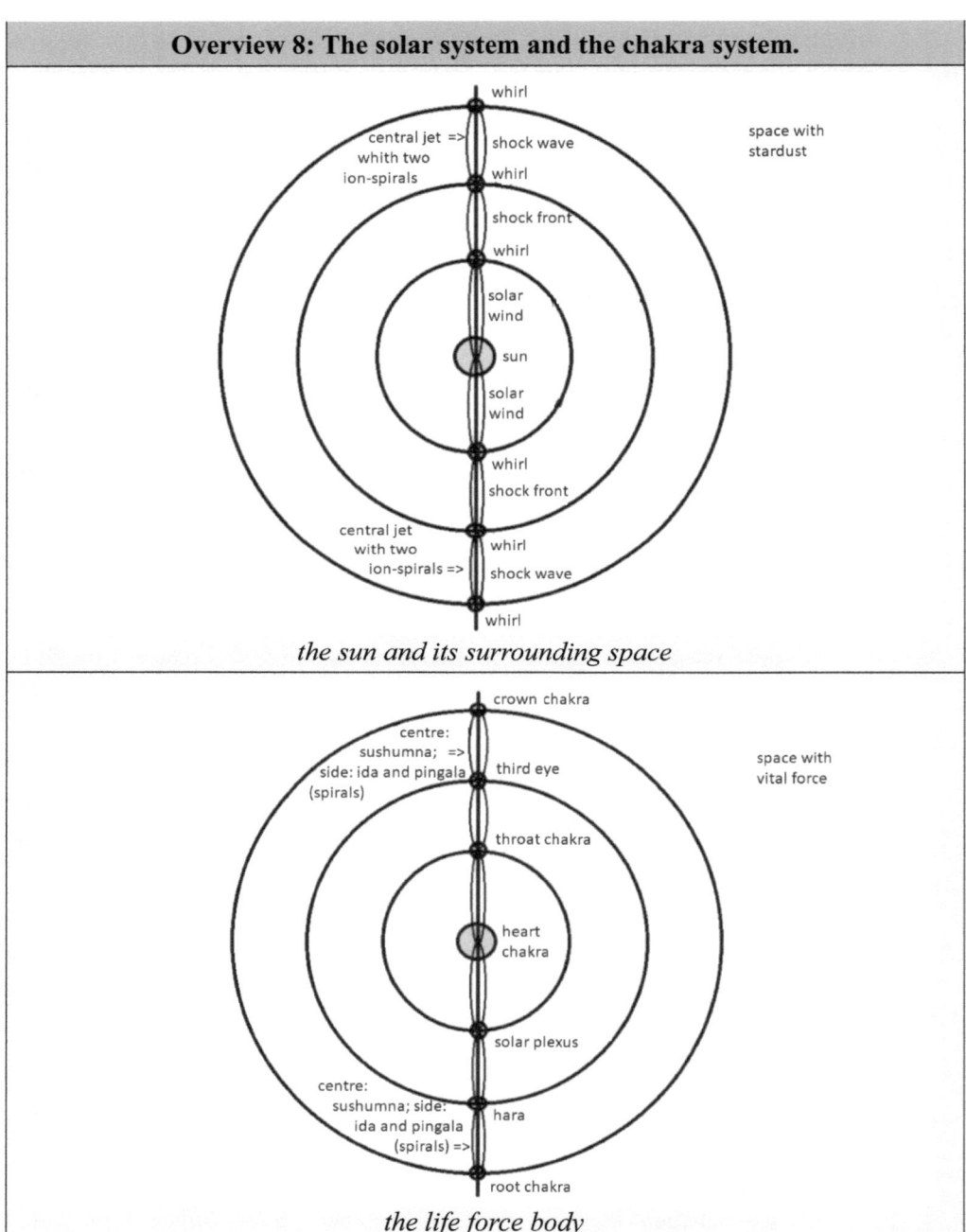

the sun and its surrounding space

the life force body

All three basic forces are involved in the process that leads to this structure in and around the sun:

Gravity pulls the stardust together to form a sun, in the center of which a high pressure is created because of its large mass, which is pulled together by gravity.

This high pressure (gravity) sets a nuclear fusion, thus a color force process, in motion, whereby the energy released thereby is radiated outward – the sun begins to shine. The photons and ions emitted in this process give rise to the solar wind space, the shock front and the bow wave.

The electrically charged particles in the rotating sun create a magnetic field, which is bundled into a jet at each of the two poles of the sun. These two jets accelerate the positively and negatively charged ions in two spiral paths around this jet, whose directions of rotation are opposite to each other. This jet/spiral structure is an effect of the electromagnetic force.

This structure is also found in an Indo-Tibetan symbol: the vajra.

Vajra

It has a spherical center that expands symmetrically in opposite directions (sun, heart chakra).

The first expansion are the two lotus flowers (solar wind space, solar plexus / throat chakra).

The new emerging form are the four elephant heads each emerging from the lotus (shock front, hara / third eye).

The touch is represented by the meeting of the four elephant trunks on the outside (bow wave, root chakra / crown chakra). The two rods in the center of the elephant heads correspond to the two jets of the sun and the sushumna.

Originally, the vajra was a symbol of lightning among the Indo-Europeans and the Neolithic peoples in Mesopotamia. It is also known from the magic wands of the Germanic seers, from the Hittites and from the Sumerians and Babylonians.

It is not possible to conclude from this symbol and its long history that people in Neolithic times already knew the chakra system or even the solar wind, but it seems as if the idea that the world originated from a unity ("Tao") by polarization into two opposites ("Yin and Yang"), and likewise that things evolve in three steps from a center (the eight "trigrams" of the I Ching), was already very old.

- - -

From the analogy between the chakra system and the solar system two important conclusions arise:

- In the center of the space around the sun is the sun, so in the center of the chakra system there must also be a "sun" – that is the soul.

The sun is the cause of the threefold structured environment of the sun (solar wind, shock front, bow wave) – without the sun this structure would not exist at all. So, by analogy, there must be such a "sun" also in the heart chakra – the soul.

- The solar system and also the chakra system are by their structure an expansion from a center, which leads in three steps to a concretization.

Since the chakra system is the basic structure of the psyche and thus of the consciousness of man, it follows from this dynamic of radiation, expansion and self-expression that this very dynamic of expansion is also the basic dynamic of the soul.

Overview 9: The Symmetry of the Chakras							
crown chakra	social contact	ecstasy					
third eye	social structure	waking consciousness					
throat chakra	social impulse	subconscious mind					
heart chakra	identity	deep sleep consciousness					
solar plexus	physical impulse	subconscious mind					
hara	physical structure	waking consciousness					
root chakra	physical contact	ecstasy					

VIII 4.   Reincarnation

For the consideration of reincarnation, the "golden thread" which could hold the different lives together has been missing up to now.

The possibility of remembering the life of a person who once lived in a former time is based on the "memory" of the collective subconsciousness. What has been missing up to now is the clear assignment of several successive lives to each other.

This clear assignment to each other also does not result necessarily from the (attempted) proof of a soul in the last chapter, but the proof of the soul makes it conceivable that different lives are "associatively connected" with each other - as this is also the case with all other contents in the individual subconsciousness and in the collective subconsciousness. The soul would then be the "golden thread" in these associations.

It would be quite astonishing if the life-memories of the deceased people would not coordinate with each other to larger forms, when all other units in the collective subconsciousness do so …

IX   The Power of Consciousness

From the previous considerations it is clear that the possibilities of consciousness to shape one's own life and the world in general in a direct way are hardly used so far. The people who do this are known as magicians, seers, healers or the like and are thought to be something exotic, which cannot be really explained and which is also not accessible for "normal people".

This means that many people do not exploit their actual potential at all ...

The possibilities of consciousness may be distinguished in two ways:

- Does consciousness work internally or externally?

- Does consciousness act on consciousness or on matter?

This results in four possibilities on which consciousness can act:

Overview 10: The possibilities of consciousness to act.			
		Where does it act?	
		internal	*external*
What does it affect?	*Consciousness*	thinking, dreaming, concentration, imagination etc.	hypnosis, telepathy, transferring consciousness into another body etc.
	Matter	understanding and curing diseases, telekinetically amplify-ing body power etc.	telepathy, telekinesis, directing chance, magic etc.

Magic consists of "two plus one" element:

- telepathy   = ability to perceive
- telekinesis   = ability to act
- analogies   = the use of analogies

These three things can be increased until they become something that is considered fundamentally different from normal telepathy, normal telekinesis, and normal use of analogies. This increase is achieved by becoming internally free of contradiction, that is, by being in tune with one's soul.

Overview 11: The increase of magic	
Initial state *(Yesod)*	*Increasing state* *(Tiphareth)*
normal telepathy	100% telepathy = astral travel
normal telekinesis	100% telekinesis = magic
normal analogy use	100%-analogy-use = being in harmony with one's soul

This state of magic can be increased a second time by establishing not only internal coordination but also external coordination. Thereby not only the individual subconsciousness becomes conscious, but also the collective subconsciousness. In doing so one goes on the Tree of Life from Yesod to Tiphareth to Da'ath – thus "ordinary magic" becomes "extraordinary magic".

The forms of magic arising from this expansion sound a bit exaggerated, but one can find reports about them in the boigraphies of famous magicians, saints, yogis and the like. Ultimately, of course, one must find out by one's own experience whether these possibilities actually exist.

Overview 12: The Two Increases of Magic		
Initial state *(Yesod)*	*1st state of increase* *(Tiphareth)*	*2nd state of increase* *(Da'ath)*
normal telepathy	100% telepathy = astral projection	omniscience
normal telekinesis	100% telekinesis = magic	miracles (materializations, walking on water etc.)
normal use of analogies	100% use of analogies = being in harmony with one's soul	being in harmony with the world (God)

English Books by Harry Eilenstein

- Living Magic (261 p.)
- The Synthesis of Physics and Magic (192 p.)
- Telepathy for Beginners (60 p.)
- Telepathy for Advanced Learners (52 p.)
- Telekinesis for Beginners (56 p.)
- Life Force for Beginners (76 p.)
- Astral Projection for Beginners (60 p.)
- Meditation for Beginners (60 p.)
- Prophecy for Beginners (60 p.)
- Ritual Magic for Beginners (64 p.)
- Magic Chant for Beginners (108 p.)
- Invocations for Beginners (52 p.)
- Evocations for Beginners (62 p.)
- Auto-Movement for Beginners (60 p.)
- Elves for Beginners (56 p.)
- Hypnosis for Beginners (56 p.)
- Love Magic for Beginners (52 p.)
- Money Magic for Beginners (60 p.)
- Magic Objects for Beginners (64 p.)

- Shamanism for Beginners (52 p.)
- Chakra-Magic for Beginners (148 p.)
- Language of the Moon – for Beginners (128 p.)
- Self Knowledge for Beginners (60 p.)
- Da'ath-Magic for Beginners (64 p.)
- Astrology for Beginners (112 p.)
- Number Symbolism for Beginners (64 p.)
- Mandalas for Beginners (76 p.)
- Crop Circles for Beginners (344 p.)
- Feng Shui for Beginners (96 p.)
- Magic Research for Beginners (140 p.)

These books will be puplished soon:

- Kundalini for Beginners
- Magic for Beginners – Anthology I
- Magic for Beginners – Anthology II
- Magic for Beginners – Anthology III
- Magic for Beginners – Anthology IV

Bücher von Harry Eilenstein

Religion allgemein
- Die sieben Schritte des Lebens (428 S.)
- Muttergöttin und Schamanen (168 S.)
- Göbekli Tepe (472 S.)
- Die Göttin von Göbekli Tepe (144 S.)
- Die Biographie des Teufels (144 S.)
- Totempfähle (440 S.)
- Christus (60 S.)
- Dakini (80 S.)
- Vajra (76 S.)

Ägypten
- Hathor und Re 1: Götter und Mythen im Alten Ägypten (432 S.)
- Hathor und Re 2: Die altägyptische Religion – Ursprünge, Kult und Magie (396 S.)
- Isis (508 S.)

Indogermanen
- Die Entwicklung der indogermanischen Religionen (700 S.)
- Wurzeln und Zweige der indogermanischen Religion (224 S.)

Germanen
- Die Götter der Germanen (87 Bände – siehe nächste Seite)
- Odin (300 S.)

Kelten
- Cernunnos (690 S.)
- Taliesin (228 S.)
- Der Kessel von Gundestrup (220 S.)
- Der Chiemsee-Kessel (76)

Psychologie
- Über die Freude (100 S.)
- Das Geheimnis des inneren Friedens (252 S.)
- Das Beziehungsmandala (52 S.)
- Gefühle und ihre Verwandlungen (404 S.)
- einsgerichtet (140 S.)
- Liebe und Eigenständigkeit (216 S.)
- Von innerer Fülle zu äußerem Gedeihen (52 S.)

Heilung
- Die Symbolik der Krankheiten (76 S.)

Kunst
- Herz des Tanzes – Tanz des Herzens (160 S.)

Drama
- König Athelstan (104 S.)

Bücher von Harry Eilenstein

„Magie für Anfänger"

- Telepathie für Anfänger (60 S.)
- Telepathie für Fortgeschrittene (52 S.)
- Telekinese für Anfänger (52 S.)
- Lebenskraft für Anfänger (60 S.)
- Meditation für Anfänger (56 S.)
- Kundalini für Anfänger (100 S.)
- Hypnose für Anfänger (56 S.)
- Auto-Movement für Anfänger (56 S.)
- Chakra-Magie für Anfänger (148 S.)
- Astralreisen für Anfänger (56 S.)
- Astrologie für Anfänger (120 S.)
- Ritual-Magie für Anfänger (56 S.)
- Mandalas für Anfänger (68 S.)
- Geldzauber für Anfänger (56 S.)
- Liebeszauber für Anfänger (52 S.)
- Invokationen für Anfänger (52 S.)
- Evokationen für Anfänger (60 S.)
- Elfen für Anfänger (56 S.)
- Magie-Forschung für Anfänger (140 S.)
- Selbsterkenntnis für Anfänger (52 S.)
- Zahlensymbolik für Anfänger (60 S.)
- Die Sprache des Mondes – für Anfänger (116 S.)
- Zaubergesänge für Anfänger (100 S.)
- Zukunftschau für Anfänger (60 S.)
- Schamanismus für Anfänger (52 S.)
- Magische Gegenstände für Anfänger (68 S.)
- Da'ath-Magie für Anfänger (64 S.)
- Kornkreise für Anfänger (348 S.)
- Feng Shui für Anfänger (96 S.)
- Magie für Anfänger – Sammelband I (696 S.)
- Magie für Anfänger – Sammelband II (664 S.)
- Magie für Anfänger – Sammelband III (580 S.)

„Traumreisen"

- Traumreisen zu Heilpflanzen (700 S.)

Magie

- Handbuch für Zauberlehrlinge (408 S.)
- Tarot (104 S.)
- Physik und Magie (184 S.)
- Die Synthese von Physik und Magie (200S.)
- Die Magie-Formel (156 S.)
- Krafttiere – Tiergöttinnen – Tiertänze (112 S.)
- Schwitzhütten (524 S.)
- Mythen und Magie der Harfe (116 S.)
- Magie heute – Berichte aus der Praxis (288 S.)

Meditation

- Der Lebenskraftkörper (230 S.)
- Die Chakren (100 S.)
- Das Chakren-System mit den Nebenchakren (296 S.)
- Organe und Chakren (64 S.)
- Die platonischen Körper in den Chakren (156 S.)
- Meditation (140 S.)
- Drachenfeuer (124 S.)
- Kundalini I (676 S.)
- Reinkarnation (156 S.)
- einsgerichtet (140 S.)

Astrologie

- Astrologie (496 S.)
- Photo-Astrologie (428 S.)
- Die astrologischen Aspekte (88 S.)
- Horoskop und Seele (120 S.)

Kabbala

- Kursus der praktischen Kabbala (150 S.)
- Eltern der Erde (450 S.)
- Blüten des Lebensbaumes:
  - Die Struktur des kabbalistischen Lebensbaumes (370 S.)
  - Der kabbalistische Lebensbaum als Forschungshilfsmittel (580 S.)
  - Der kabbalistische Lebensbaum als spirituelle Landkarte (520 S.)

Die Themen der 87 Bände der Reihe „Die Götter der Germanen"

1. Die Entwicklung der germanischen Religion
2. Lexikon der germanischen Religion
3. Der ursprüngliche Göttervater Tyr
4. Tyr in der Unterwelt: der Schmied Wieland
5. Tyr in der Unterwelt: der Riesenkönig Teil 1
6. Tyr in der Unterwelt: der Riesenkönig Teil 2
7. Tyr in der Unterwelt: der Zwergenkönig
8. Der Himmelswächter Heimdall
9. Der Sommergott Baldur
10. Der Meeresgott: Ägir, Hler und Njörd
11. Der Eibengott Ullr
12. Die Zwillingsgötter Alcis
13. Der neue Göttervater Odin Teil 1
14. Der neue Göttervater Odin Teil 2
15. Der Fruchtbarkeitsgott Freyr
16. Der Chaos-Gott Loki
17. Der Donnergott Thor
18. Der Priestergott Hönir
19. Die Göttersöhne
20. Die unbekannteren Götter
21. Die Göttermutter Frigg
22. Die Liebesgöttin: Freya und Menglöd
23. Die Erdgöttinnen
24. Die Korngöttin Sif
25. Die Apfel-Göttin Idun
26. Die Hügelgrab-Jenseitsgöttin Hel
27. Die Meeres-Jenseitsgöttin Ran
28. Die unbekannteren Jenseitsgöttinnen
29. Die unbekannteren Göttinnen
30. Die Nornen
31. Die Walküren
32. Die Zwerge
33. Der Urriese Ymir
34. Die Riesen
35. Die Riesinnen
36. Mythologische Wesen
37. Mythologische Priester und Priesterinnen
38. Sigurd/Siegfried
39. Helden und Göttersöhne
40. Die Symbolik der Vögel und Insekten
41. Die Symbolik der Schlangen, Drachen und Ungeheuer
42.a Die Symbolik der Herdentiere I
42.b Die Symbolik der Herdentiere II
43. Die Symbolik der Raubtiere
44. Die Symbolik der Wassertiere und sonstigen Tiere
45. Die Symbolik der Pflanzen
46. Die Symbolik der Farben
47. Die Symbolik der Zahlen
48. Die Symbolik von Sonne, Mond und Sternen
49.a Das Jenseits I – Das Hügelgrab
49.b Das Jenseits II – Der Jenseitsweg
50. Seelenvogel, Utiseta und Einweihung
51. Wiederzeugung und Wiedergeburt
52. Elemente der Kosmologie
53. Der Weltenbaum
54. Die Symbolik der Himmelsrichtungen und der Jahreszeiten
55.a Mythologische Motive I
55.b Mythologische Motive II
56. Der Tempel
57. Die Einrichtung des Tempels
58. Priesterin – Seherin – Zauberin – Hexe
59. Priester – Seher – Zauberer
60. Rituelle Kleidung und Schmuck
61. Skalden und Skaldinnen
62 Kriegerinnen und Ekstase-Krieger
63. Die Symbolik der Körperteile
64.a Magie und Ritual I
64.b Magie und Ritual II
64.c Magie und Ritual III
65. Gestaltwandlungen
66.a Magische Angriffs-Waffen
66.b Magische Verteidigungs-Waffen
67. Magische Werkzeuge und Gegenstände
68. Zaubersprüche
69. Göttermet
70. Zaubertränke
71. Träume, Omen und Orakel
72. Runen
73. Sozial-religiöse Rituale
74. Weisheiten und Sprichworte
75. Kenningar
76. Rätsel
77. Die vollständige Edda des Snorri Sturluson
78. Frühe Skaldenlieder
79.a Mythologische Sagas I
79.b Mythologische Sagas II
80. Hymnen an die germanischen Götter